www.wadsworth.com

www.wadsworth.com is the World Wide Web site for
Thomson Wadsworth and is your direct source to
dozens of online resources.

At *www.wadsworth.com* you can find out about
supplements, demonstration software, and student
resources. You can also send email to many of our
authors and preview new publications and exciting
new technologies.

www.wadsworth.com
Changing the way the world learns®

Current Perspectives
Readings from InfoTrac® College Edition on Social Policy
and Developmental Psychology

CAMILLE ODELL
Utah State University

with

MICHELL M. VLAHOS and **JANIE MAXFIELD**
Utah State University

THOMSON
™
WADSWORTH

Australia • Brazil • Canada • Mexico • Singapore • Spain •
United Kingdom • United States

THOMSON

WADSWORTH

**Current Perspectives: Readings from InfoTrac® College Edition
on Social Policy and Developmental Psychology
Camille Odell, Michell M. Vlahos, and Janie Maxfield**

Acquisitions Editor: *Michele Sordi*
Assistant Editor: *Daniel Moneypenny*
Editorial Assistant: *Kara Warren*
Technology Project Manager: *Lauren Keyes*
Marketing Manager: *Sara Swangard*
Marketing Assistant: *Natasha Coats*
Marketing Communications Manager: *Linda Yip*
Project Manager, Editorial Production: *Samen Iqbal*
Creative Director: *Rob Hugel*

Print Buyer: *Linda Hsu*
Permissions Editor: *Sarah D'Stair*
Production Service: *Ruchika Vij, Interactive
   Composition Corporation*
Cover Designer: *Larry Didona*
Cover Image: *Photolibrary.com/Photonica*
Cover Printer: *Thomson West*
Compositor: *Interactive Composition Corporation*
Printer: *Thomson West*

Library of Congress Control Number:
2006931052

ISBN: 0-495-17062-3

For more information about our products,
contact us at:
**Thomson Learning Academic Resource Center
1-800-423-0563**

For permission to use material from this text
or product, submit a request online at
http://www.thomsonrights.com.
Any additional questions about permissions
can be submitted by e-mail to
thomsonrights@thomson.com.

Contents

Author's Introduction

for

Current Perspectives: Readings from InfoTrac® College Edition on Social Policy and Development for Developmental Psychology

(This reader will accompany Shaffer and Kipp's Developmental Psychology, 7ᵗʰ Edition)

The study of child and adolescent human development is universally one of the most compelling topics that a college student undertakes. Students find this topic inherently interesting because such an undertaking provides for self-reflection and scrutiny of personal experience. Using a global perspective, my students often come to agree with me when I say that children are the world's greatest resource—a resource that we have tools to protect and nourish, or to squander through ignorance.

Issues surrounding development during childhood and adolescence have never been more gripping or complicated. *Current Perspectives: Readings from InfoTrac College Edition on Social Policy and Development for Developmental Psychology* was created to provide students using Shaffer's and Kipp's excellent *Developmental Psychology* text with an opportunity to explore some of these issues through case studies and the most recent findings of today's researchers. The 15 articles included in this reader have been selected from a compendium of outstanding sources available on Thomson's InfoTrac College Edition. Each article has been chosen in keeping with my desire to provide cutting edge, research-based information about some of today's hottest topics in child and adolescent development.

I've drawn heavily on the opinions of my students as I've made my selections. Beyond providing sound research findings on hot topics, each article was carefully screened to ensure that the piece is engaging, readable, and provocative. I use the word provocative because I place high value on encouraging and honing critical thinking skills in students.

This Reader is arranged in a sequence that is loosely tied to the pattern of human development, beginning with issues surrounding fertility and conception, and ending with teenage issues of cutting and steroid use. However, I encourage you to read the articles in the order you find to be most interesting to you.

Questions at the end of each article were created to challenge you to address the topic on a personal level and to encourage you to assess your understanding of the topics covered.

Happy reading!

Camille Odell

Last Chance Family

Couples Plagued With Infertility Find a New Path to Parenthood: Adopting Frozen Embryos

Richard Jerome

Byline: Richard Jerome Joanne Fowler in Houston and Los Angeles and Ron Arias in Los Angeles

Eager to have children, Tom and Karen Sperling began trying as soon as they were married in December 1994. But that joyful task would turn into a long and anguished struggle. For five years, despite hormone injections and artificial insemination, Karen was unable to conceive: She could not produce viable eggs. "Month after month, hope starts to fade," says the 36-year-old homemaker from the Chicago suburb of Hillside, who was so consumed by the effort that she quit her job as an administrative assistant.

A friend finally offered to act as an egg donor, but Karen graciously declined. "I didn't feel comfortable with my husband and somebody else making this child together," she says. Adoption appeared to be the most realistic alternative, but for Karen even that was a dispiriting prospect. "Ever since I was a little girl, I'd wanted to experience pregnancy," she says. "It was like a big part of me was being taken away."

Then she found a new source of hope: embryo adoption. In recent years a small but increasing number of clinics storing the unused embryos of couples who have conceived through in vitro fertilization (IVF) have begun embryo donation services. With their clients' permission, they offer surplus embryos to infertile couples who crave the full childbearing experience—except, of course, for the fact that the baby will not be biologically theirs. "It isn't all that different from a traditional adoption," says Dr. Stanley Korenman, associate dean for Ethics and Medical Scientist Training at UCLA, who supports the idea. "It's just that they adopt the child nine months earlier." One contrast is that embryo adoption can cost recipients as little as $3,000 as opposed to $25,000 for the average traditional adoption. On the other hand the results are far from guaranteed. Only 60 percent of frozen embryos survive the thawing process and just 20 percent of those transferred yield offspring.

Those odds were good enough for the Sperlings. Scouring the Internet, Karen learned of an embryo donation program at the University of Iowa. In the summer of 1999 she and Tom, 37, a carpenter, drove to Iowa City, where they underwent medical and psychological evaluations. They then received profiles of four potential donors, unidentified except for their ethnicity and three generations of medical history. They settled on a couple with a heritage similar to their own—a mix of German, English, Irish and Polish—who had stored six embryos for seven years and signed away all rights to them. "We hoped for children who looked like they came from us," Karen explains. After giving her two months of hormone injections, doctors implanted half the embryos into her fallopian tubes. The procedure failed, and the Sperlings all but gave up hope.

But on Dec. 3, 1999—their fifth wedding anniversary—doctors at Iowa made a last-ditch effort, implanting Karen with the rest of the embryos. Two weeks later, the clinic called with the results of a blood test: She was pregnant. "We were wandering around on cloud nine," she says, "but I kept waiting for the other shoe to drop." Make that two: On Aug. 9, 2000, she gave birth to twin sons, 8-lb. Logan and 6 1/2-lb. Ryan. Four days later, Karen brought the boys home. "I had them in the cradle that once belonged to my great-grandfather," she remembers. "I just stood there looking at their little fingers, hands and faces."

Few would begrudge her maternal rapture. Nevertheless, embryo adoption remains uncharted—and largely unregulated—territory. The practice, introduced in the mid-'90s, is an outgrowth of the burgeoning fertility-treatment industry, which has served roughly 9 million American women. Of those, fewer than 5 percent opt for IVF, in which the woman's eggs are fertilized in a test tube and the resulting embryos are implanted in her uterus. In most cases, couples stockpile more embryos than they need and keep the extras frozen until they decide what to do with them. An estimated 150,000 languish at about 400 clinics nationwide. Many scientists hope that one day these embryos can be used for research on stem cells—those cells whose growth could one day be controlled in the lab and targeted to replace or restore specific damaged tissue or even whole organs. At present, however, almost all the embryos wind up being discarded.

Putting those embryos up for adoption, which has so far resulted in dozens of successful births, raises significant practical and moral questions. "In terms of legal implications, everyone should sign contracts in which they define who is going to raise the kids and what parental rights the donors have," says Korenman. "It's so much better to have all questions on the table at the beginning than to start squabbling over them years later." Harder to determine is what's best for the baby-to-be. Should donor couples have any contact with children born of their adopted embryos? Should embryo-adopted children learn anything of their forebears or whether they have siblings in another family? "It could be problematic for children never to know their genetic parents," says medical ethicist George Annas, professor of health law at Boston University. Andrea Bonnicksen, a Northern Illinois University political science professor who follows the issue, agrees that the children should bond with donor parents, but adds, "It's difficult to predict the feelings that might unexpectedly arise. It's advisable to proceed with care and caution."

Arguments over embryo adoption also intersect with the national debate over embryonic stem cell research, which, advocates believe, could offer hope to those who suffer from Parkinson's, spinal cord injury and other grave afflictions. Worthy as that goal is, critics, who include the Pope, say the means of achieving it are immoral. And embryo donors often come from the ranks of those who hold such views. "They feel there is life from conception," says Charlotte Danciu, a Boca Raton, Fla., adoption attorney. "They don't want their embryos dissected for scientific research."

Ron and Sandra Elliott, who recently moved from the Houston area to Anacoco, La., are a case in point. Pentecostal Christians, they wed in September 1990 and soon faced a reproductive morass. The father of two sons from a first marriage, Ron had to reverse a vasectomy so the pair could have children. Then Sandra suffered two ectopic pregnancies—the embryos lodged in the fallopian tubes, one of which ruptured. In March 1996, Sandra began in vitro treatments. The Elliotts deposited nine unused embryos in the Fertility Center of San Antonio. The fate of any surplus embryos was far from their minds. "We thought we might have to use them," says Sandra, 40, a homemaker. "At the time, you just want that baby."

Nine months after starting IVF, Sandra delivered healthy triplets: Alexandra, Amanda and Joshua. That was family enough for the Elliott budget, leaving the unused embryos in cold storage. Three years passed, until the clinic wrote the couple to ask if they wanted to renew their contract, donate the embryos for research or discard them. "I didn't want to flush them down the drain," says Ron, 45, an Army Reserves major and media relations officer at Fort Polk, La. Then Sandra saw a magazine article about Snowflakes, a five-year-old embryo adoption program run by Nightlight Christian Adoptions of Fullerton, Calif. Says Sandra: "This was the answer to our prayers."

Snowflakes encourages a wide-open approach to embryo adoption. Donors and recipients exchange "life books," with photos and essays on family lifestyle and history. The Elliotts chose a middle-aged couple from Northern California. "They shared Bible verses with us, so it was clear God was their top priority," says Sandra. Adds Ron: "If I couldn't raise those kids, they were the perfect family to do it."

After both sets of parents signed a contract (stipulating, among other things, that the donors must receive at least one picture a year of any resulting children), the clinic packed the embryos in canisters filled with liquid nitrogen and shipped them to California. Nine months later, the recipient mother was pregnant. By then the couples were chatting by phone, the mom-to-be bubbly with enthusiasm. But the openness proved too much for Sandra, who found herself tormented by the idea that someone else would bear her child. "To be perfectly honest," she says, "part of me was hoping the embryos wouldn't take."

In December 2000 the recipient bore a healthy baby boy. When she began sending the Elliotts letters and photographs, "I bawled," says Ron, "thinking that maybe we made a mistake." Then last July the Elliotts went to California, with butterflies in their stomachs, to meet the child. To their surprise, the encounter helped them let go. "He was a happy little cuddly baby," Sandra remembers. "That gave me a lot of peace. I didn't feel crushed that I couldn't take him home—I can say that from the bottom of my heart."

In another case Southern California embryo recipients Wendy and Steve Strong will avoid such a complicated family reunion. Their donors preferred anonymity. Married in 1992, the Strongs had struggled mightily with a range of fertility problems before the birth of their son Matthew, now 6. "We hoped the miracle would happen again," says Wendy, 42, who like her husband is a teacher. Conceiving a second child, however, was even tougher. Fertility treatments failed completely. Then, in November 1999, a pregnant single woman approached the Strongs through mutual friends and asked if they would be interested in adopting her child. Wendy, an adoptee herself, leaped at the chance.

After the baby girl was born, the mother brought her several times to visit the Strongs, who had decorated a room with a crib. But four hours before the adoption was scheduled to be finalized, the woman changed her mind. The deeply religious couple—Wendy once worked as a missionary in the South Pacific—absorbed the blow sadly but philosophically. "It was heartbreaking," says Steve, 32. "But it wasn't supposed to happen, and we accept that." Recalls Wendy: "Steve said if God wants us to have another child, someone will offer another one on the phone. I thought he was almost crazy."

Not quite. The next month, January 2000, a nurse called from nearby Huntington Reproductive Center, the Strongs' fertility clinic. "A couple wants to donate four embryos," she said. "I know in my heart they are perfect for you." The anonymous donors had expressed a wish that the recipients share their European ancestry, and the Strongs filled the bill.

Though they knew little about embryo adoption, Wendy and Steve researched it on the Internet and agreed to the arrangement. They paid a $2,500 administrative fee for the transfer of the embryos, while the donors signed away all legal and parental rights to any potential children. For about two weeks, Wendy took estrogen and progesterone injections that prepared her uterine lining to accept the embryos, which were implanted in March 2000. Within 12 days she learned she was pregnant, and on Nov. 29, she gave birth to 8 1/2-lb. Caleb—named for a Biblical figure of unshakable faith—who announced his arrival with an aria of deafening screams. "It's so amazing," marvels Wendy, "that he was once in a petri dish."

The Strongs don't intend to keep his origins secret from their younger son. "I always want him to know of our desire to have a family and the miracle of how God brought him to us," Wendy says. "Who knows? Maybe some of his contemporaries at school will say, 'Oh, yeah, I was part of an embryo adoption too.'"

For now, however, the reaction from others is often puzzlement. Recently, Wendy was lounging with Matthew and Caleb at a Pasadena swim club when, after scrutinizing them for several minutes, a man noted that the baby bore no resemblance to his mother and big brother. "He must look like your husband," the stranger said. Normally Wendy either explains that Caleb is adopted or attempts a short lecture on embryo adoption. But not this time. "No, he doesn't," she replied. "He is his own person."

QUESTIONS

1. What is embryo adoption? What are the chances of having children through this method?
2. What kinds of legal or moral problems may arise with embryo adoption?
3. How will the practice of embryo adoption contribute to the nature vs. nurture debate surrounding human development?

2

The Shape of Your Baby's Head—Cause for Concern or Common?

Barbara S. Greenstreet

As an Early Interventionist, I am often approached by parents with questions and concerns about their baby's development. Recently, Diane stopped in to my office, with her three month old baby in her arms.

"Just look at the shape of her head!" she exclaimed with concern. "It's totally FLAT on the back! Do you think she's OK?"

Diane is not alone in her worry. Over the last several years, pediatricians have seen an increase in the number of infants with this condition, which may be called positional or occipital plagiocephaly, or cranial asymmetry. It simply means that the head is shaped unevenly, usually with a flattened area on the back or one side of the skull. Recently, most cases of the irregularity are traceable to a safe and healthy reason: "Back To Sleep."

Since 1992, when the American Academy of Pediatrics first publicized its recommendation that infants be put to sleep on their backs—supine, rather than prone—parents and their children's doctors have reported an increase of babies with "funny shaped heads," as parents often express it.

The Back To Sleep habit has significantly reduced incidents of Sudden Infant Death Syndrome (SIDS), by 40% according to some reports, and this is great news. But one side effect is that infants tend to have the same part of their head against the flat mattress every night, as well as during naps, and they often develop a flatter area there. (Bald spots are also common, but resolve as new hair grows in.)

In fact, this cranial asymmetry can occur for several different reasons, including position in the womb or short, tight or sore neck muscles; in addition to the back-sleeping.

Pediatrician Dr. Stephen Tarzynski, Assistant Chief of Pediatrics at Kaiser-Permanente Health Center's West Los Angeles facility, comments, "A baby's head is like a water balloon. We're finding a lot of babies who are getting flat heads in back."

Just how serious is this problem? Many parents are concerned that the flattening may affect brain development, and either cause or be a sign of a disability. Dr. Nancy Shinno, co-director of the Kaiser Craniofacial/Cleft Palate Team (Kaiser-Permanente, Southern California) writes, "This asymmetry will not cause any brain damage. The major problem that results from such a head shape is that one ear is usually farther in front than the other ear, and this may make it difficult for your child to wear glasses later in life."

When should a parent be concerned? How much flattening is still "within normal" and at what point should you consult your baby's doctor about this?

Of course, you should always contact your child's doctor right away about any concern, including the shape of your baby's head. The doctor should take head measurements at regular well-baby check-ups to ensure normal head growth.

Dr. Roger Knapp, a pediatrician in private practice in Southlake, Texas, adds that if he has not seen the infant turn its head to each side, "I ask the parents at the two week checkup, 'Can the baby turn its head both ways?' I also notice if the baby cries when I turn the head to the side."

In fact, no one has a perfectly round or oval, symmetrical head. As the baby's hair fills in, and the body grows to become more proportionate with head-size, the irregular shape becomes less noticeable. Also, the shape normalizes more once the baby has matured enough to move its head freely, lift its head easily from the surface, and to turn over or roll independently. Typically, by about eighteen months of age the head has attained more of the expected roundness or symmetry.

Still, there are several techniques recommended to help your baby's head develop more evenly, and to reduce the flatness if it has already appeared.

Dr. Tarzynski of Kaiser-Permanente explains, "To prevent flattening we recommend turning the baby on his/her belly for about an hour a day (it can be three times for 20 minutes, four times for 15 minutes, etc.) while being watched closely by the parent. This seems to mitigate the asymmetry from that cause."

Many developmental experts agree and some advise even more time spent in the prone (tummy-down) position each day. Kathy Ludlow, OTR/L, a pediatric motor therapist in North Bend, Washington, urges parents to give their babies plenty of "tummy-time" during waking hours each day. "This is important not only for head shape, but also for general development of body strength, and fine and gross motor skills."

The American Academy of Pediatrics has noted that attainment of infant gross motor milestones (sitting independently, crawling) does appear to occur slightly later in infants who sleep on their backs as opposed to side or front-sleeping, although the lag resolves by eighteen months. More parents report later crawling, and in some cases no crawling at all, in their back-sleeping babies.

Ludlow emphasizes, "A generous portion of time spent playing on the floor will ensure that babies use their hands, arms, and full-body muscles to move and explore." Car seats, swings, 'exercise saucers' and infant carriers have their usefulness, but," says Ludlow, "every baby needs daily time without the support of these types of equipment to develop their muscles, as well as to allow for even head development."

Breast-feeding naturally encourages parents to hold the baby on each side, which helps with even head growth. If you are bottle-feeding, be sure to do the same, either at each feeding or alternating feedings, change which arm you cradle the baby with to vary the direction the baby faces.

Drs. Nancy Shinno and Andrew Wexler of the Craniofacial Team at Southern California Kaiser-Permanente offer these guidelines to parents, to reduce the uneven pressure on the baby's head:

- Alternate the placement of mobiles, toys and other objects of interest near the baby's crib, so that he or she will turn in different directions to see them.

- Switch your baby's position in the crib (which end of the mattress the head is toward), so that he will have to turn the other way to look at you (especially if you sleep in the same room), the door, or the room in general.

- Use variations in car seats and strollers as well: hang toys or objects of interest on different sides at different times. If an older sibling frequently rides in the car with the baby, alternate which side of the car seat he or she sits on, as the baby is likely to turn in that direction.

- Let baby be on his stomach as much as possible when awake (with your close observation).

- When your baby has developed good head control, the occasional use of a 'jumper,' swing, or saucer will give your baby variety without added pressure to the head.

Occasionally, if these measures are not enough to prevent or resolve any flattening, a special helmet may be prescribed to mold the skull into a more rounded shape. The baby generally must wear the helmet 23 hours per day, seven days a week, taking it off primarily for bathing. Usually a few weeks to a few months with the helmet therapy will correct the problem.

Remember that no one is perfectly symmetrical in head-shape or in other features of the body. "I wear two different shoe sizes!" comments Dr. Knapp, of Texas. Often a baby's head shape is as much the result of inherited traits as it is positioning.

Diane, who was reassured by her pediatrician that her baby's head was rounding out nicely on its own, realized that several people on her husband's side of the family had similarly squarish heads, when she looked closely. "At least she's a girl!" she laughs, brushing her baby's wispy infant hair. "We'll just let her have longer hair, or even curl it a bit, to camouflage the flat spot, if she still has one!"

Barbara S. Greenstreet, M.A., is a freelance writer and Early Intervention Specialist with over 20 years' experience teaching infants, toddlers and preschoolers with developmental delays and disabilities, and counseling families of children with special needs. She lives with her husband and three teenagers in western Washington State, and writes frequently on parenting and child development topics.

QUESTIONS

1. What is the "Back to Sleep" campaign and what have been its effects: Generally? On SIDs deaths? On meeting motor milestones?

2. Name 5 ways to reduce uneven pressure on a baby's head.

3. When is "tummy time" encouraged, and why is it important?

3

The Case for Staying Home

Caught Between the Pressures of the Workplace and the Demands of Being a Mom, More Women Are Sticking With the Kids

Claudia Wallis

Byline: Claudia Wallis with reporting by Esther Chapman/Omaha, Wendy Cole and Kristin Kloberdanz/Chicago, Lauren Comiteau/Amsterdam, Helen Gibson and Jennie James/London, Terrence Murray/Paris, Ulla Plon/Copenhagen, Julie Rawe/New York, Betsy Rubiner/Des Moines, Ursula Sautter/Bonn, Sonja Steptoe/Los Angeles and Deirdre van Dyk/Arlington

On a crisp spring morning in the smart English town of Cambridge, Helen Powell, 33, is having the time of her life. In a 60-minute span, she blows up a paddling pool, rescues assorted plastic dinosaurs from the outskirts of her garden, makes a cake out of Play-Doh, and builds a boat with some brightly colored, oversized plastic bricks. In the living room, Powell's two sons—Jack, 5, and Tom, 3—are on a tear, thumping on the piano before joining their mother in the boat for a spot of make-believe seafaring. "Management consultancies should send their consultants to families for training," says Powell, taking a sip of tea as her sons head into the garden. "A mother can time-manage like nobody on earth."

Six years ago, Powell was a pensions solicitor with a Big Six law firm in the City of London, while her husband pursued an accounting career. But when she was three months pregnant, Powell became worried about her quality of life and grew weary of "stomach-clenching deadlines." So she decided to focus solely on being a mother, and walked away from her $76,000-a-year career.

Now, in addition to running her family and a community playgroup, she also oversees a local toy library. "Weirdly," she says, "the things I did as a solicitor prepared me [for other things] in all sorts of unexpected ways. The diplomacy one has to exercise when dealing with clients is similar to the negotiating skills required for dealing with toddlers." With Jack now in his first year at school and Tom just 18 months away from that milestone, Powell occasionally thinks about going back to work. Every so often she gets an e-mail from someone at her old firm, telling her how much they'd like her to. But she has doubts. "Even if you get offered fixed hours, that just means you probably can go home at 6 p.m.," she says. "You're still out of the house for all your children's waking hours." Her big concern is what she might miss during office hours. Last January, after a snowfall, she picked up Jack from school on a blue plastic sled. "The stars were out, the moon was out," she says. "It was a golden time. I'm sure I will go back to work, but it's going to be hard because of the hours." A high-powered career, she laments, "is full-time or nothing."

Ten, 15 years ago, it all seemed so doable. Bring home the bacon, fry it up in a pan, split the second shift with some sensitive New Age man. But slowly the snappy, upbeat work-life rhythm has changed for professional women like Powell. Sure, European countries have given women the right to maternity leave and, sometimes, generous subsidies for child care, and France has even instituted a 35-hour workweek. But for European executives, the norm is still 50 hours a week for women and 55 for men, according to Catalyst, a U.S.-based research and consulting group that focuses on women in business. For top executives in big corporations in the U.S., it's 60 to 70 hours a week. For dual-career U.S. couples with kids under 18, the combined work hours have grown from 81 a week in 1977 to 91 in 2002, according to the Families and Work Institute.

E-mail, pagers and cell phones promised to allow execs to work from home. Who knew that would mean that home was no longer a sanctuary? Today BlackBerrys sprout on the sidelines of children's soccer games. Cell phones vibrate at the school play. It's back to the e-mail after the bedtime story. And this particular reality is as globalized as business itself. When it comes to the obstacles faced by female business executives in both Europe and the U.S., says Meredith Moore, Catalyst's director of research, "we were surprised by how little variation there was."

Meanwhile, the pace has quickened on the home front, where a mother's job has expanded to include managing a packed schedule of child-enhancement activities. In their new book *The Mommy Myth*, Susan Douglas, a professor of communication studies at the University of Michigan, and Meredith Michaels, who teaches philosophy at Smith College, Massachusetts, label the phenomenon the New Momism. Nowadays, they write, the culture insists that "to be a remotely decent mother, a woman has to devote her entire physical, psychological, emotional and intellectual being, 24/7, to her children." For most mothers—and fathers, for that matter—there is little choice but to persevere on both fronts to pay the bills. Indeed, 72% of mothers with children under 18 are in the U.S. workforce—a figure that is up sharply from 47% in 1975 but has held steady since 1997. In Germany, the proportion of mothers between 15 and 64 who are working is 64%.

But in the professional and managerial classes, where higher incomes permit more choices, a reluctant revolt is under way. Today's women execs are less willing to play the juggler's game, especially in its current high-speed mode, and more willing to sacrifice paychecks and prestige for time with their family. Like Powell, most of these women are choosing not so much to drop out as to stop out, often with every intention of returning. Their mantra: You can have it all, just not all at the same time.

Their behavior, contrary to some popular reports, is not a 1950s embrace of old-fashioned motherhood but a new, nonlinear approach to building a career and an insistence on restoring some kind of sanity. "What this group is staying home from is the 80-hour-a-week job," says sociologist Arlie Hochschild, author of *The Time Bind: When Work Becomes Home and Home Becomes Work.* "They are committed to work, but many watched their mothers and fathers be ground up by very long hours, and they would like to give their own children more than they got. They want a work-family balance."

Since women in the U.S. normally take six to 12 weeks of maternity leave—much of it unpaid—before returning to work, they often feel that longer leave and more flexible working hours would help keep women satisfied and on the job. It's different in Europe, where governments have been trying to legislate some sanity into the work-family equation for several decades. Maternity leave in Britain is now 12 months—with new moms receiving up to full pay for the first six. In Sweden, parents can share up to 16 months' leave after a birth, with up to 80% pay. But because of competitive pressure, few people take the full entitlement. Stockholm-based asset manager Annika Svensson, 34, returned to work 13 months after the birth of both of her children. "Even if I wanted to," she says, "I felt I had no choice but to go back to work. [Otherwise,] there would be a man at the starting gate waiting to take my job."

In Germany, where mothers can return to their jobs up to three years after giving birth—and in some circumstances may even take the third year of this leave up until their child's eighth birthday—many women would like to get back to work but stay at home because of the lack of child-care facilities. For example, in western Germany child-care places outside the home exist for only 2.7% of children younger than 3, so many mothers have little choice but to stay with the kids. As a result, only 32.3% of mothers of children under 3 are working. The figure rises to 66.2% for mothers of children aged between 6 and 10 who are in school.

Because the American female professionals who are opting out represent a small and privileged sector, the dimensions of the exodus are hard to measure. What some experts are zeroing in on in the U.S. is the first-ever drop-off in workplace participation by married mothers with a child less than 1 year old. That figure fell from 59% in 1997 to 53% in 2000. The drop may sound modest, but, says Howard Hayghe, an economist at the U.S. Bureau of Labor Statistics, "that's huge," and the figure was roughly the same in 2002. Significantly, the drop was mostly among women who were white, over 30 and well educated.

U.S. Census data reveal an uptick in stay-at-home moms who hold graduate or professional degrees—the very women who seemed destined to blast through the glass ceiling. Now 22% of them are home with their kids. A study by Catalyst found that 1 in 3 women with M.B.A.s are not working full-time (it's 1 in 20 for their male peers). Economist and author Sylvia Ann Hewlett, who teaches at Columbia University in New York City, says she sees a brain drain throughout the top 10% of America's female labor force (those earning more than $55,000). "What we have discovered in looking at this group over the last five years," she says, "is that many women who have any kind of choice are opting out."

Other experts say the dropout rate isn't climbing but is merely more visible now that so many women are in high positions. In 1971 just 9% of medical degrees, 7% of law degrees and 4% of M.B.A.s were awarded to women in the U.S.; 30 years later, the respective figures were 43%, 47% and 41%. European figures are harder to come by, but Catherine Hakim, a sociologist at the London School of Economics, says the trend is "particularly relevant to the younger generation." Says Cisca Dresselhuys, 60, editor in chief of the Dutch feminist monthly *Opzij*: "My generation started it. Now we see our daughters having all these choices we didn't have. What do you choose? You can choose it all, but that's too much for one person."

THE GENERATION FACTOR

For an older group of female professionals like Dresselhuys, who came of age listening to Helen Reddy roar, the exodus of younger women can seem disturbingly regressive. Fay Clayton, 58, a partner in a small Chicago law firm, watched in dismay as her 15-person firm lost three younger women who left after having kids, though one has since returned part time. "I fear there is a generational split and possibly a step backward for younger women," she says.

Others take a more optimistic view. "Younger women have greater expectations about the work-life balance," says Joanne Brundage, 51, founder and executive director of Mothers & More, a mothers' support organization with 7,500 members and 180 chapters in the U.S. While boomer moms have been reluctant to talk about their children at work for fear that "people won't think you're a professional," she observes, younger women "feel more entitled to ask for changes and advocate for themselves." Brundage may be ignoring that young moms can afford to think flexibly about life and work while pioneering boomers first had to prove they could excel. "The younger generation doesn't feel they have to prove they can do it," says Hakim. "They are saying, 'This is no way to live. What's the point of having all this money if you can't enjoy any kind of normal family life?'"

One woman in Brussels, who doesn't want to be identified by name, knew that her promising career as an E.U. lawyer was on "skid row" when she decided to work part time so she could take care of her children. So she left her job for seven years; when she went back, she found it unfulfilling and eventually quit again. She has "no doubt" that without children, she would be earning a higher salary in a more prestigious job. But she disagrees with the conventional definition of hard work and achievement. "I don't know many women who think it's an achievement to sit in an office and fly around the world for 80 hours a week," she says. "I don't regard that as achievement, and I think that most women would regard it as imbecilic." Much of career ambition, she adds, "is simply vanity. Wanting that title or that company car, but who cares?" Raising children, she says, is "where you have real power and influence over the future of the world."

A 2001 U.S. survey by Catalyst of 1,263 men and women born between 1964 and 1975 found that Gen Xers "didn't want to have to make the kind of trade-offs the previous generation made. They're rejecting the stresses and sacrifices," says Catalyst's Paulette Gerkovich. "Both women and men rated personal and family goals higher than career goals." Catalyst plans to conduct a similar survey in Europe next year.

A newer and larger survey, conducted late last year by the Boston-area marketing group Reach Advisors, provides more evidence of a shift in attitudes. Gen X (which it defined as those born between 1965 and 1979) moms and dads said they spent more time on child rearing and household tasks than did boomer parents (born between 1945 and 1964). Yet Gen Xers were much more likely than boomers to complain that they wanted more time. "At first we thought: Is this just a generation of whiners?" says Reach Advisors president James Chung. "But they really wish they had more time with their kids." In the highest household-income bracket ($120,000 and up), Reach Advisors found that 51% of Gen X moms were home full time, compared with 33% of boomer moms. But the younger stay-at-home moms were much more likely to say they intended to return to work: 46% of Gen Xers expressed that goal, compared with 34% of boomers.

Chung and others speculate that the attitude differences can be explained in part by forces that shaped each generation. While boomer women sought career opportunities that were unavailable to their mostly stay-at-home moms, Gen Xers were the latchkey kids and the children of divorce. Also, their careers have bumped along in a roller-coaster, boom-bust economy that may have shaken their faith in finding reliable satisfaction at work.

Pam Pala, 35, of Salt Lake City, Utah, spent years building a career in the heavily male construction industry, rising to the position of construction project engineer with a big firm. But after her daughter was born 12 months ago, she decided to stay home. "I grew up in a divorced family. My mom couldn't take care of us because she had to work," she says. "We went to baby-sitters or stayed home alone and were scared and hid under the bathroom counter whenever the doorbell rang." Pala wants to return to work when her daughter is in school, and she desperately hopes she won't be penalized for her years at home. "I have a feeling that I'll have to start lower on the totem pole than where I left," she says. "It seems unfair."

MATERNAL DESIRE AND DOUBTS

Despite such misgivings, most women who step out of their careers find expected delights on the home front, not to mention the enormous relief of no longer worrying about shortchanging their kids. Six years ago, life for Danish author Lotte Garbers, now 36, became intolerable. Back then, she was a high-flying executive, running Microsoft Denmark by day and splitting the nursery run with her husband in the evening to collect the couple's two sons, Rasmus, now 11, and Jonas, now 8. "I found out I didn't like this life at all," says Garbers, who left the corporate world to stay at home. She now has three novels to her name and a laptop humming quietly in one corner of the family's sun-filled home in Espergaerde, 40 km north of Copenhagen. In the living room, Jonas and a friend have made a tent by draping a blanket over chairs arranged in a circle. Each time it collapses, Garbers helps rebuild it. "I can't imagine going back to the career track," she says. "It would require a programmed life from early morning to late evening. I like my kids to have peaceful days, together and with me."

Others appreciate a slower pace and being there when a child asks a tough question. In McLean, Virginia, Oakie Russell's son Dylan, 8, recently inquired, out of the blue, "Mom, who is God's father?" Says Russell, 45, who gave up a dream job as a TV executive: "So, you're standing at the sink with your hands in the dishwater and you're thinking, 'Gee, that's really complicated. But I'm awfully glad I'm the one you're asking.'" Psychologist Daphne de Marneffe speaks to these private joys in a new book, *Maternal Desire*, to be published in Britain in September. De Marneffe argues that feminists and American society at large have ignored the basic urge that most mothers feel to spend meaningful time with their children. "Anyone who has tried to 'fit everything in,'" she writes, "can attest to how excruciating the five-minute wait at the supermarket checkout line becomes, let alone a child's slow-motion attempt to tie her own shoes when you're running late getting her to school." The book puts an idyllic gloss on staying home. But it could launch a thousand resignations.

What De Marneffe largely omits is the sense of pride and meaning that women often gain from their work. Women who step out of their careers can find the loss of identity even tougher than the loss of income. After her twin sons were born six years ago, Paris-based financial auditor Agathe Berge, 34, transferred departments within Arthur Andersen to cut down on her workload. Then, when baby Charles came along two years later, she opted for part-time work within the company. But she missed her children. "I just was not seeing them grow up and that was always on my mind," she says. In 2003, she dropped out altogether. She was happy about having more time with her children, but she also found herself nostalgic for her working identity. So she's currently seeking part-time employment. "It's really not about working for money or power, but also to exist. In today's society, being a stay-at-home woman can be looked down upon," she says.

"I don't regret leaving, but a huge part of me is gone," says Bronwyn Towle, 41, who surrendered a demanding job as a Washington lobbyist to be with her two sons. Now when she joins her husband, Raymond, who works at the U.S. Chamber of Commerce, at work-related dinners, she feels sidelined. "Everyone will be talking about what they're doing," says Towle, "and you say, 'I'm a stay-at-home mom.' It's conference buzz kill." Last year, after her youngest child went to kindergarten, Towle eased back into the world of work. She found a part-time job in a forward-thinking architectural firm, but hopes to return to her field eventually. "I wish there was more part-time or job-sharing work," she says.

It's a wish expressed by countless formerly working moms in the U.S. But in much of Europe, it's a reality. In the 1980s in the Netherlands, the government began encouraging part-time work as a way of tackling unemployment. Part-time workers were given the same benefits and access to training and education as full-time workers. Now, 20% of Dutch men and 73% of Dutch women work part time, compared with the U.S., where just 17% of moms with a child under 18 work part time. There are more part-time workers in the Netherlands than anywhere else in the industrialized world. And the part-time option has become so popular, in fact, that 10% of young Dutch parents now both opt to work four days a week. After Amsterdam-based journalist Pieternel Gruppen, 32, had her daughter Kika 2 1/2 years ago, both she and her partner, Tobias Baardman, downshifted into a four-day week. "It was an easy decision," says Gruppen. "Weekends alone would not be long enough to spend with my daughter." Baardman, whose weekends now begin on Thursday afternoon, feels the same way: "I'm absolutely happy. I can make a serious career and still have enough time to do other things in my life."

Not all Europeans are comfortable with the part-time track. "I'm convinced that if I asked for reduced time, I'd be transferred to less important and interesting work," says Swedish mother Svensson. European fathers, too, are wary of using paternity leave for fear of losing ground to office rivals.

BUILDING ON-RAMPS

Hunter college sociologist Pamela Stone has spent the past few years interviewing 50 stay-at-home mothers in seven U.S. cities for a book on professional women who have dropped out. "Work is much more of a culprit in this than the more rosy view that it's all about discovering how great your kids are," says Stone. "Not that these mothers don't want to spend time with their kids. But many of the women I talked to have tried to work part time or put forth job-sharing plans, and they're shot down. Despite all the family-friendly rhetoric, the workplace for professionals is extremely, extremely inflexible."

That's what Ruth Marlin, 40, of New York City found even at the family-friendly International Planned Parenthood Federation. After giving birth to her second child 16 months ago, she was allowed to ease back in part time. But Marlin, an attorney and a senior development officer, was turned down when she asked to make the part-time arrangement permanent. "With the job market contracted so much, the opportunities just aren't there anymore," says Marlin, who hates to see her $100,000 law school and undergraduate education go to waste: "Back in the dotcom days, people just wanted employees to stay. There was more flexibility."

There are signs that in some corners things are changing. In Britain since April 2003, employers must consider requests for flexible working hours from parents of children under 6—although they are not legally obliged to honor all such requests. In industries that depend on human assets, serious work is being done to create more part-time and flexible positions. At the U.S.-based PricewaterhouseCoopers (PWC), 10% of the firm's female partners are on a part-time schedule, according to the accounting firm's chief diversity officer, Toni Riccardi. And, she insists, it's not career suicide: "A three-day week might slow your progress, but it won't prohibit you" from climbing the career ladder. PWC is hardly alone. Last February New York City-based economist Hewlett convened a task force of leaders from 14 companies and four law firms to discuss what she calls the hidden brain drain of women and minority professionals. "We are talking about how to create off-ramps and on-ramps, slow lanes and acceleration ramps," so that workers can more easily leave, slow down or re-enter the workforce, she explains.

"This is a war for talent," says Carolyn Buck Luce, a partner at the accounting firm Ernst & Young, who co-chairs the task force. Over the past 20 years, half of new hires at Ernst & Young have been women, she notes, and the firm is eager not only to keep them but to draw back those who have left to tend to their children.

This spring Deloitte Touche Tohmatsu will launch a Personal Pursuits program, allowing above-average performers to take up to five years of unpaid leave for personal reasons. Though most benefits will be suspended, the firm will continue to cover professional licensing fees for those on leave and will pay to send them for weeklong annual training sessions to keep their skills in shape. Such efforts have spawned their own goofy jargon. Professionals who return to their ex-employers are known as boomerangs, and the effort to reel them back in is called alumni relations. One reason businesses are getting serious is demographics. With boomers nearing retirement, a shortfall of perhaps 10 million workers appears likely by 2010 in the U.S.

Will these programs work? Will part-time jobs really be part time, as opposed to full-time jobs paid on a partial basis? Will serious professionals who shift into a slow lane be able to pick up velocity when their kids are grown? More important, will corporate culture evolve to a point where employees feel genuinely encouraged to use these options? Anyone who remembers all the talk about flex time in the 1980s will be tempted to dismiss the latest ideas for making the U.S. workplace family-friendly. But this time, perhaps, the numbers may be on the side of working moms—along with many working dads who are looking for options, too.

On-ramps, slow lanes, flexible options and respect for all such pathways can't come soon enough for mothers eager to set examples and offer choices for the next generation. Terri Laughlin, 38, a stay-at-home mom and former psychology professor at the University of Nebraska at Lincoln, was alarmed a few weeks ago when her daughters Erin, 8, and Molly, 6, announced their intentions to marry men "with enough money so we can stay at home." Says Laughlin: "I want to make sure they realize that although it's wonderful staying at home, that's only one of many options. What I hope to show them is that at some point I can re-create myself and go back to work." With reporting by Esther Chapman/Omaha, Wendy Cole and Kristin Kloberdanz/ Chicago, Lauren Comiteau/Amsterdam, Helen Gibson and Jennie James/ London, Terrence Murray/Paris, Ulla Plon/Copenhagen, Julie Rawe/New York, Betsy Rubiner/Des Moines, Ursula Sautter/Bonn, Sonja Steptoe/Los Angeles and Deirdre van Dyk/Arlington

"I CAN'T IMAGINE GOING BACK TO THE CAREER TRACK. I LIKE MY KIDS TO HAVE PEACEFUL DAYS, TOGETHER AND WITH ME."—LOTTE GARBERS, Danish author

QUESTIONS

1. What is the "stop out" phenomenon? Why is it an advantage over "drop out" for individuals and for the business environment?

2. How will on ramps and off ramps help with the problem of the "hidden brain drain" of women and minority professionals?

3. Why are businesses getting serious about "brain drain" being created by female professionals to leaving their careers to stay home with their children?

4

Fathers and Attachment

In this article, Anthony Curtis reviews the role of fathers in childcare and attachment and considers the case for a re-examination of the complementary roles of parenthood.

Tony Curtis

Welcome to the world of the father, where nothing is as it was. You may think you know now what it is to have responsibility, to be tired and wan, to be torn between the demands of the personal and professional, to be unable to get anything organised because of the busy-ness of your hectic life. But let me assure you as one who knows. I can safely promise you that at present you know nothing at all. And yet you are not only a man to be pitied, an innocent babe about to discover the true meaning of the word care. You are also to be envied—the luckiest man alive.

Peter Howarth's Foreword
in *Fatherhood: An Anthology
of New Writing* (1998)

The above quotation captures many of the shared beliefs and experiences, not to mention hopes and fears, when we first become parents. My own recent baptism into this role has given me a richness and purpose of role (not to mention a sense of wonder about it all) that is hard to put into words. I know a little more than "nothing at all," as Peter Howarth suggests, but I'm still proudly wearing my L-plates!

The experience of attending antenatal classes before Olivia was born equipped us well in terms of knowing what to do when the waters break, or how some babies decide to come out breach. What they don't teach you is how to cope with and adapt to the emotional roller-coaster that inevitably accompanies parenthood, or how best fathers in particular can or should be involved in childcare. Love, it seems, does not prepare us all to be brilliant dads.

THE ROLE OF FATHERS

The role and status of fathers in the Western model of childcare is at best recognised as an optional extra to motherhood and at worst ignored and patronised by critical writers of variable parenting experience. It is true that times are changing (and have changed) during the last 30 years in particular, and attitudes, beliefs and practices along with them. In the 1950s and 1960s, for example, fathers were discouraged from attending hospital deliveries. Today they are encouraged not only to attend but also to actively participate in all aspects of pre- and post-natal activities, including the delivery itself.

Research by Lewis (1986) showed that fathers who attended their child's birth did not appear to differ significantly from those who did not in terms of their subsequent involvement in childcare at home. Mothers still predominantly did the childcare, feeding, nappy changing, getting up at night if the precious one was fretting (the baby not the father!) At least two factors seem to contribute to this. First, the father will more often be in longer employment (Lewis found that fathers contributed more if the mother was working). Secondly, it is easy for fathers to feel marginalised in baby care; mothers are seen as the "experts" in this role (a view that is often reinforced by health-care professionals and mothers themselves who retain their own areas of "expertise"). Such assumptions present missed opportunities for fathers to demonstrate their own latent skills and talents along the road to fatherhood.

FATHERS AND PSYCHOLOGY

A review of the psychological literature suggests that you need not be a rocket scientist to recognise the traditional marginalisation and devaluation of the role of fathers in childcare. Paradoxically, in terms of the wider concept of parenthood, psychodynamic research into the long-term effects of early experience of childhood indicates a much greater role for fathers in terms of protecting against long-term disturbance in adulthood (Rutter 1981). Similarly, Erikson implicitly includes paternal faith in his psychosocial theory with the development of trust which fathers can provide in terms of enhancing total security.

In addition, fathers may also provide a unique role in pulling children out of symbiotic fusion with their mothers and thereby allow for their psychological birth and autonomy (Geiger and Newman 1996). This may be evidenced in fathers stimulating their children's increasing level of skill development or providing a stabilising influence uncontaminated by ambivalence towards the mother (that is, infants simultaneously wanting to be a part of and apart from their mother).

Despite these and other findings, Bowlby's monotropy theory of attachment (which maintains that the mother's attachment is qualitatively different to all other attachments) suggested that the father is of no direct emotional significance to the young infant but only of indirect value as an emotional and economic support for the mother (Gross et al. 2000). Similarly, Margaret Mead, the social anthropologist, once famously asserted that fathers were "a biological necessity but a social accident." Advances in medical technology, together with insights from contemporary psychological research, have challenged both of these descriptions and prompted psychologists to re-examine the role of fathers in childcare.

Schaffer and Emerson (1964) demonstrated that children can and do often form multiple attachments with caregivers (including fathers), contrary to Bowlby's theory, and that an infant's emotional dependence on a caregiver is not related to the caregiver's continued presence. What is more important, they argued, is the sensitivity of the caregiver to the infant's needs (which could quite easily be satisfied in many cases by the father). In addition, there are individual differences in battles and caregivers that must also be considered. For example, some children like cuddling while others do not. Equally, there are different kinds of attachment, each of which is important for healthy development.

Other research supports this view, suggesting that the mother and father are both important attachment objects for their infants but the circumstances that lead to selecting each may differ. A father's style of play is often more physically stimulating and unpredictable, whereas mothers are more likely to hold their infants, soothe them, attend their needs and read stories (Lamb 1981).

EVOLUTIONARY EXPLANATIONS

3NCL FATHERS

Evolutionary psychologists see mothers as having greater parental investment in their offspring, and hence being better prepared for child-rearing and attachment (Kenrick 1994). Essentially, parental investment refers to any investment by the parent in an individual offspring that increases the offspring's chances of survival (and hence reproductive success) at the cost of the parent's ability to invest in other offspring. The optimum or ideal number of offspring may differ for each parent (for example, for many mammals a low-investing male will have the potential to sire more offspring than a single female could produce). The father's role in this context does not differ markedly from that of Margaret Mead's statement above (that is, males are necessary for the continuation of the species).

Explanations of childcare and attachment behaviours are best understood in terms of providing the child with protection and nurture. Attachment from both the father's and mother's viewpoint is essential to ensure that the carrier of their genetic investment is looked after. Genes that instruct both parents to take care with their offspring will tend to thrive and spread since they will be found in that offspring (Cartwright 2001). However, such views may be criticised as being reductionist in nature and difficult to test and therefore disprove.

CROSS-CULTURAL RESEARCH
AND FATHERS

Cross-cultural research into the role of fathers has shown that fathers can fulfil a parenting role just as well as mothers (for example, in single-parent father families) but that typically fathers do not have such a large part in child-rearing and domestic tasks as mothers (Lamb 1987). The highest degree of father involvement in childrearing in any human society is by the Aka pygmies, a hunter-gatherer people in the Central African Republic. Fathers were found to be present with an infant or child 88% of the time, and to be holding an infant 22% of the time. This high degree of physical intimacy by fathers is further enhanced by the overlapping subsistence activities of both genders. Women often assist in the hunting and men often carry the infants back after the hunt. Even in this society, however, mothers still engage in more childcare than fathers.

Similarly, the dominant role of women in childcare is found in the African Efe tribe from Zaire who live in extended family groups. Infants are looked after by many carers (and even breast-fed by different women) but usually sleep with their own mother at night.

Recent research has suggested a cultural shift towards equal status roles of fathers and mothers in childcare in many cultures. In Sweden, these cultural trends are further supported in legislation that encourages fathers to take paternity leave and promotes equality between mothers and fathers in terms of work opportunities. Advertising campaigns were promoted nationally to increase paternal involvement in care.

In the UK, similar recent legislation has allowed fathers increased paternity leave to promote their greater involvement in childcare. However, legislation takes time to bring about changes in long-established gender differences (and beliefs) in childcare. Although the idea of the new, nurturant father is not entirely mythical, the largest observed changes have been shown in the period following the birth of the baby (getting up for the baby at night) rather than bathing and nappy changing!

So rather than being a poor substitute for a mother, fathers make their own unique contribution to the care and development of infants and young children (at least in two-parent families). The picture that emerges is that the

father's role is complementary and different rather than unnecessary and defi-
cient. The challenge for psychology is to demonstrate how fathers best fit in
to this long neglected role.

DOES "NEW MAN" EXIST?

The "dual-earner couples" phenomenon (where the husband works full-time
and the wife works at least 20 hours per week) has become quite common,
particularly in the UK and USA. Compared with more traditional couples,
these husbands report more marital dissatisfaction and conflicts over family
and work responsibilities, and the wives similarly report higher levels of conflict, as well as a very realistic work overload (Gross 2001). Despite evidence
that childcare tasks are more evenly shared in some dual-earner families, it is
nearly always the woman who is still primarily responsible for both house-
work and childcare, regardless of the age of the children and whether she
works full-time or part-time. A recent survey in the UK found that 82% of
husbands had never ironed, 73% had never washed clothes, and 24% had never
cooked. It would appear, in this context at least, that new man is still rather
shy to leave his traditional cave.

On a more positive note, a recent meta-analysis of 24 studies in the USA
suggests that fathers' participation in their children's activities is increasing. Fathers' engagement with their children (that is, interactions such as playing,
reading and helping with homework) increased from 34% (mid-1960s to early
1980s) to 43% (mid-1980s onwards), as a percentage of their mothers' engagement. In addition, their availability (how much time they spend near their
children, whether interacting or not) also increased by a similar amount, from
52% to 66% (again, as a percentage of their mothers' engagement) for the
same period. What this study fails to show, however, are the changing ways in
which fathers relate to, and interact with, their children over this period. More
qualitative research is required to extend and complement these findings.

ALTERNATIVE RELATIONSHIPS

Recent trends in family life (for example, the dissolution of the traditional nuclear family, increases in divorce, out-of-wedlock childbearing) mean that now
only about half of all children in the UK grow up in homes with two biological, married parents. Alternative family arrangements include step-parents and
lesbian and gay parenting. In terms of the former, young people living in step-
families in New Zealand had increased risks of poor psychosocial outcomes,
including substance abuse, leaving school without qualifications or engaging
in early sexual activity (Gross 2001). However, a re-examination of these findings showed that confounding social, contextual and individual factors that

operated prior to the formation of the stepfamily were more likely to be responsible for these poor outcomes.

Similar findings from children in lesbian and gay households have found that such children are no more at risk of poor social outcomes, once the psychological distress of earlier marital breakdowns has been accounted for. It is difficult therefore to identify which family groupings produce which kinds of relationship effects.

FATHERS AND DIVORCE

What is clear, however, is that while married fathers are engaging more with their children than they used to, most divorced fathers have little or no contact with their children, and an increasing number of men remain unmarried. Furthermore, some fathers deny responsibility for their children and this collectively leads to more children living without resident fathers. The long-term consequences of father absence are not yet known (for both children and their parents).

SUMMARY

This article has attempted to highlight the imbalance that currently exists, both within psychology and in wider disciplines, in understanding the importance and role of fathers in childcare and development. More research is required to establish the importance of fathers and fatherhood in a field that has traditionally been dominated by the importance and value of mothers and motherhood. Crucially, more ambitious and sensitive research is required to look at the ways in which these two changing roles best complement and interact with one another. This is necessary not only for the emotional security of our future children but also for us as developing parents. We cannot afford to overlook fathers.

Anthony Curtis is Education and Training Manager with Wiltshire Shared Services NHS Consortium and Honorary Lecturer at the University of Bath. He is also a Senior Examiner for a major examining board, an Editor of Psychology Review and father to Olivia.

REFERENCES

Cartwright, J. H. (2001) *Evolutionary Explanations of Human Behaviour*, Routledge Modular Psychology Series.

Geiger, B. and Newman, J. (1996) *Fathers as Primary Caregivers*, Greenwood Press.

Gross, R. D. (2001) *Psychology: The Science of Mind and Behaviour*, 4th edn, Hodder and Stoughton.

Gross, R. D., McIlveen, R., Coolican, H., Clamp, A. & Russell, J. (2000) *Psychology: A New Introduction for A2,* Hodder and Stoughton.

Howarth, P. (ed.) (1998) *Fatherhood: An Anthology of New Writing*, Indigo.

Kenrick, D. T. (1994) "Evolutionary Social Psychology: From Sexual Selection to Social Cognition," *Advances in Experimental Social Psychology*, Vol. 26, pp. 75–121.

Lamb, M. E. (1981) "The Development of Father-Infant Relationships," in M. E. Lamb (ed.) *The Role of the Father in Child Development,* Wiley.

Lamb, M. E. (1987) *The Father's Role: Cross-Cultural Perspectives*, Lawrence Erlbaum.

Lewis, C. (1986) *Becoming a Father*, Oxford University Press.

Rutter, M. (1981) *Maternal Deprivation Reassessed*, 2nd edn, Penguin.

Schaffer, H. R. and Emerson, P. E. (1964) "The Development of Social Attachments in Infancy," *Monographs of the Society for Research in Child Development*, Vol. 29, No. 3.

TEACHERS' NOTES

A site that includes topics ranging from expectancy to vasectomy and dedicated to the relatively neglected area of fatherhood is: http://www.lapas.org/.

This site is largely for the lay-person but has some very useful information mixed in with the pop quizzes and videotapes. Try the Fatherhood link to Transitions and Griefs for a thoughtful article by two experienced therapists and fathers, Randy Mergler and Roger Coughlan.

An interview with Dr Susan Maushart on motherhood (mentioned in Richard Gross's column in the last issue) can be found at: http://www.mothersandmore.org/Features/Maushart_interview.htm

QUESTIONS

1. How do the play styles of fathers and mothers differ? How might these differences be complementary? How might they cause problems?

2. What is "parental investment," according to evolutionary psychologists?

3. What evidence is there that father's participation in their children's activities is increasing?

5

Spanking: A Slap at Thoughtful Parenting

Barbara J. Howard

wonder if more pediatricians would discuss spanking with new parents if they knew that 25% spank infants who are only 1–6 months old or that half of them spank children before their first birthday.

Seventy-seven percent of mothers and 71% of fathers hit their 1-year-olds. That's a huge amount of spanking at an age when it is clear that the child is not old enough to understand the lesson the parent is trying to teach.

As children get older, spanking gets worse. It is more common and has more side effects. Ninety percent of 3-year-olds get spanked. We know that in order to be effective, a painful stimulus has to be increased to maintain its effectiveness over time. We also know that toddlers and preschoolers misbehave every 6–8 minutes. So it is not surprising that there is going to be a lot of hitting, and it's likely to get more intense once spanking is in the parents' disciplinary repertoire.

Hitting doesn't stop, even when parents believe that it should. Sixty percent of children aged 10–12 years, 40% of those aged 14 years, and 25% of those aged 17 years are still being hit by their parents.

Does it get your attention to know that even parents who advocate spanking admit that 50% of the times they've done it, it was an inappropriate reaction for the offense? Or, that children who are spanked become more aggressive, are less attentive to social cues, are more likely to have delinquent behavior outside the home, and are more likely as adults to approve of spanking and to hit their spouse than peers who are not spanked?

Spanking is a knee-jerk reaction, even though research tells us it is no more effective than non-painful forms of discipline that are less harmful to the child in the short term and the long term. Parents spank because they were spanked.

I don't throw a lot of data at parents. I discuss spanking with them as I would a decision about using a medication: Here's what it does, here's what we know about the side effects, and here are the alternatives.

Don't tell parents that spanking doesn't work, or they will stop listening to you. That's because it looks like it works at the moment. When you spank a child, he or she is no longer participating in whatever behavior prompted the swat but is crying instead. The chance of him or her going back to the behavior is likely regardless of the consequence that is given, because that is what childhood learning is like: repetitious.

I ask parents whether they would be interested in learning about alternative disciplinary strategies that work just as well as spanking, but without the side effects. It's important and not that hard to broach the subject in a non-threatening, nonjudgmental way.

If a parent brings up a behavioral problem, I simply ask, "How do you handle that? How is that for you?" and "How bad does it get?" Some of the side effects are easy for parents to see. I'll ask, "Has he hit you yet?" or "How does he get along with other children?"

It helps to be empathetic, to show that you understand how difficult parenting can be. Then your offer to help will be more welcome. I listen and watch for what they're doing well and build on that. So I point out examples that I just observed or that they just reported about parts of parenting that are going smoothly and ask, "How did you get that to go so well?" Then I analyze the components of their success, which usually include consistency limits, agreement of both parents, and clear emotions.

Using that as a base, I discuss alternatives—such as age-appropriate time-out. Time-out is a technique that involves time away from reinforcement accompanied by disapproval, loss of freedom, and loss of interesting things to do. In a 9-month-old, that can mean making an angry face, saying, "No biting!" and turning away for 15 seconds. In a toddler, it means a brief time on a chair or in the crib, again with a look of disapproval but no continued attention. In a preschool child, it means sitting in a chair. For a preteen or teenager, being grounded is time-out. I tell parents that once they establish this consequence for times it is needed, they "will never have to hit their children."

I offer strategies and a time frame in which to expect success to parents who are already spanking their children but are willing to consider a change. I ask these parents whether for 3 weeks, they can agree to use time-out for the specific occasions of aggression for which they now spank. What usually happens is that time-out starts to work. It is important to follow up by phone or with a visit to support this process.

To the parent who says, "I was hit, and I turned out okay," I may say, "Yes, I can see that you did. How is your relationship with your father now?" It is remarkable how many times the parent will confess that the relationship is distant.

If the relationship is good, I ask what other things their parent did to raise them. Usually, there are many positives. Then I can say, "It looks as though your father would have been successful with you even without spanking."

Then we talk about risk. How much does spanking increase the risk of a child becoming aggressive? The risk may be increased as much as fourfold, the research shows.

Sometimes it helps to tell parents that painful punishments make non-painful punishments less effective. Kids who are spanked at home think time-out in preschool is a joke. So parents who spank at home are potentially making it very difficult for schools to manage their children. Hearing this gets parents' attention, especially if there is already a behavior problem in school or day care.

I should warn you that you have to be careful when you talk to parents about spanking. It can be a dicey topic of conversation—right up there with race, sex, and politics.

Dr. Barbara J. Howard is assistant professor of pediatrics at Johns Hopkins University, Baltimore, where she directs residency training in behavioral pediatrics and codirects the behavioral pediatrics fellowship hip program. She also practices developmental-behavioral and general pediatrics with Potomac Physicians in Annapolis Md.

QUESTIONS

1. Why can spanking appear to be successful at training behavior? Why is the undesirable behavior likely to be repeated, despite a spanking?

2. What is an effective alternative to spanking?

3. How much does spanking increase the risk of a child becoming aggressive?

6

The Biology of Child Maltreatment

How Abuse and Neglect of Children Leave Their Mark on the Brain

The President and Fellows of Harvard College

Scientists are discovering that early experiences can have profound long-term effects on the biological systems that govern responses to stress. If these systems lack the environment required for normal development, they may fail to function as evolution designed them. Effects on the maturing brain can be subtle as well as obvious. Disturbances at a critical time early in life may exert a disproportionate influence, creating the conditions for childhood and adult depression, anxiety, and post-traumatic stress symptoms.

The body and brain adapt to acute stress—originally, a threat to survival or bodily integrity—through the activity of the hypothalamic-pituitary-adrenal (HPA) axis and the sympathetic nervous system. The hypothalamus, at the base of the brain, secretes corticotropin-releasing factor (CRF), which stimulates the pituitary gland to release adrenocorticotropic hormone (ACTH). ACTH travels to the adrenal glands and causes the release of the stress hormones cortisol and adrenaline (epinephrine), mobilizing the body and mind for fighting or fleeing. Blood pressure and blood sugar levels rise, breathing and heart rate increase, muscles tense, and we feel anger, anxiety, or fear. The system is controlled by feedback: A high level of stress hormones signals the hypothalamus to stop issuing CRF. Along with the HPA axis, the sympathetic nervous system is activated, as CRF influences circuits that use the neurotransmitters dopamine, norepinephrine, and serotonin.

If the stress response is provoked too often or for too long, it becomes less adaptive. A person under chronic stress, with no hope of relief, is constantly on guard and never able to relax, psychologically or physiologically. The feedback mechanism loses its sensitivity, and the system fails to shut off.

Depression bears some resemblance to an acute stress response that persists when it is no longer needed. The adrenal glands produce more cortisol, and an injection of the synthetic stress hormone dexamethasone often does not have the normal feedback effect of suppressing the release of cortisol. Depressed persons may have excess CRF in the spinal fluid and greater expression (activation) of genes for producing CRF receptors in the brain, especially the centers of memory and strong emotions in the hippocampus and amygdala. Instead of being temporarily and appropriately alert and vigilant, a depressed person is likely to be either chronically lethargic and apathetic or agitated, anxious, and sleepless.

It has long been known that childhood abuse and neglect and the loss of a parent are associated with adult psychiatric disorders, including depression, anxiety, and post-traumatic symptoms. Apart from heredity and recent stress, child maltreatment is the most common predictor of major depression in adults. Now researchers are discovering how early experiences affect the ability to maintain psychological and physical balance. Childhood trauma and loss can cause prolonged hypersensitivity to stress by upsetting the regulation of the HPA axis and sympathetic nervous system.

Receptors in the brain are sensitive to CRF in infancy and even before birth. A depressed mother raises the level of CRF in the child she is carrying. Six-month-old children of women who were depressed or abused while pregnant secrete cortisol at a higher than average level in response to mild stress.

Some of these effects can be demonstrated experimentally in laboratory animals. Rat pups were removed from their mothers repeatedly before weaning. The mothers tended to neglect pups treated this way, giving them little attention and feeding them last. When tested as adults, the rats overreacted to mild stress and were more likely to suffer from a rat equivalent of depression—passivity in difficult situations and a weak response to rewards like sugar water. Young hamsters placed in a cage with mature hamsters that threaten and attack them show lasting changes in the brain circuitry using serotonin and other neurotransmitters that regulate mood and aggression.

People who suffer childhood maltreatment are more vulnerable to post-traumatic stress symptoms after further traumatic childhood or adult experiences because their bodies and brains have "learned" that they cannot count on protection and solace in distressing situations. The symptoms of post-traumatic stress disorder (PTSD) include heightened anxiety and jumpiness, intrusive memories and flashbacks, avoidance of situations, places, and people reminiscent of the traumatic event, and often emotional numbness, loss of trust in others, and an aversion to intimate relationships.

PTSD is usually preceded by an acute stress reaction that involves activity of the HPA axis and sympathetic nervous system. The amygdala, the brain's center for registering fear, intensifies memories of trauma through its links to the hypothalamus, hippocampus, and cerebral cortex. The aroused amygdala strengthens connections that produce emotionally charged memories. Its function is to make these memories difficult to eradicate so that we will recognize the threat if it reappears. In this way, traumatic experiences are preserved in long-term memory, and anything even remotely reminiscent of the trauma may serve as a cue to revive the experience. Re-experiencing further strengthens the emotional associations, which in turn further consolidates the memory in a vicious cycle.

Excess cortisol production can damage the hippocampus, disrupting the connections between neurons and eventually cause the neurons themselves to degenerate. Brain-derived neurotrophic factor (BDNF), which helps the hippocampus to generate neurons, is reduced in rats who have been separated from their mothers. One study found a shrunken hippocampus in depressed women who were traumatized as children. In another study, women with post-traumatic stress disorder resulting from child abuse showed abnormal activity in the frontal lobes.

Researchers are looking for ways to prevent and reverse the harm, either in childhood or later in life. Rat pups from a genetically anxious strain respond much better to stress as adults if they are adopted by unusually attentive foster mothers who constantly lick and groom them. In a strain of rats sensitive to alcohol, the risk of addiction is increased by early separation from their mothers. Selective serotonin reuptake inhibitors (Prozac and company) may partially reverse the effect. These drugs may also promote the regeneration of neurons in the hippocampus.

Drugs that interfere with the activity of CRF are being considered for the treatment of depression. Mifepristone (RU-486), best known as an abortion drug, is a CRF antagonist that has shown some promise as a treatment for psychotic depression. Propranolol (Inderal), a drug that blocks nerve receptors for norepinephrine in the amygdala, apparently reduces arousal in response to memories of a traumatic experience when it is taken for several weeks starting immediately after the trauma. It could be warding off PTSD by preventing traumatic memories from working their way indelibly into the brain.

Psychological treatment for post-traumatic stress disorder also involves retraining the amygdala to respond differently when traumatic memories recur. And it may turn out that sometimes the nature of the childhood experience determines the choice of treatment. In one study, an antidepressant was compared to cognitive behavioral therapy and a combination of the two in the treatment of severely depressed women. The combination was best for the group as a whole, but for those who had suffered traumatic experiences in childhood, the drug was less effective than psychotherapy and the combination was no better than psychotherapy alone.

Maltreatment does not, of course, cause the same changes in neurotransmitter or stress hormone activity or long-term brain function in everyone. Individual genetic characteristics are important; for example, there is evidence that one variant of a gene that governs the reabsorption of serotonin promotes greater activity in the amygdala and makes children more vulnerable to stress.

The kind of stress—parental loss; neglect; physical, sexual, or emotional abuse—may also make a difference. And some maltreated children, instead of developing adult psychiatric disorders, come through relatively unscathed.

Learning more about the biological consequences of child maltreatment through brain imaging and molecular genetic studies will help in defining more precisely the causes and nature of depression, anxiety, and post-traumatic stress symptoms. Just as important, it may improve our understanding of how resilient children maintain hope, control anxiety, and achieve normal development despite abuse and neglect.

REFERENCES

Cicchetti D. "An Odyssey of Discovery: Lessons Learned through Three Decades of Research on Child Maltreatment," *American Psychologist* (Nov. 2004): Vol. 59, No. 8, pp. 731–41.

Glaser D. "Child Abuse and Neglect and the Brain—A Review," *Journal of Child Psychology and Psychiatry and Allied Disciplines* (Jan.–Feb. 2000): Vol. 41, No. 1, pp. 97–116.

Luecken LJ, et al. "Early Caregiving and Physiological Stress Responses," *Clinical Psychology Review* (May 2004): Vol. 24, No. 2, pp. 171–91.

Nemeroff CB, et al. "Differential Responses to Psychotherapy versus Pharmacotherapy in Patients with Chronic Forms of Major Depression in Childhood Trauma," *Proceedings of the National Academy of Sciences* (Nov. 25, 2003): Vol. 100, No. 24, pp. 14,293–96.

Sapolsky RM. *Why Zebras Don't Get Ulcers: A Guide to Stress, Stress Related Diseases, and Coping.* W.H. Freeman, 1994.

For more references, please see www.health.harvard.edu/mentalextra.

QUESTIONS

1. When can the feedback mechanism in the brain lose its sensitivity? How is depression related to this process?

2. How are traumatic memories remembered so long? What is the role of the amygdala in this process?

3. What treatment worked better for severely depressed women who suffered traumatic experiences as children? How is this outcome different from the group as a whole?

7

Girls, Boys and Autism

Is This Mysterious and Sometimes Devastating Condition Just an Extreme Version of Normal Male Intelligence? That's One Provocative New Theory. Behind Autism's Gender Gap

Geoffrey Cowley

Andrew Bacalao has a good, sharp mind. At 13, he's a decent pianist, a devotee of Frank Lloyd Wright, a master at video-games and jigsaw puzzles. He remembers phone numbers like a Pocket PC, and he can dismantle a radio or a flashlight in the time it takes some people to find the power switch. But drop in on Andrew at home in Oak Park, Ill., and you quickly sense that something is amiss. "Can you look at her?" his mom, Dr. Cindy Mears, prompts, as a *Newsweek* correspondent greets him in the living room. He stays on the couch, feet up, mesmerized by a handheld game called Bop It Extreme. Soon he's making soap bubbles and running outside to bang on the windows. Andrew does eventually talk, but conversation doesn't come easily. When his mom asks him not to burp, he tells the guest, "I'm going to unbutton your outfit." He's merely offering to take her jacket—and he seems to think his choice of words is just fine.

What do you make of such a kid? A generation ago, he might have been written off as a discipline problem or a psychopath—someone who insists on misbehaving even though he's smart enough to know better. But we now know there are different kinds of intelligence, which can crop up in unusual combinations. The world, as it turns out, is full of people who find fractal geometry easier than small talk, people who can spot a tiny lesion on a chest X-ray but can't tell a smile from a smirk. Most of these folks qualify as "autistic," but not in the traditional sense. Classic autism is a devastating neurological disorder. Though its causes are unclear, it has a strong genetic component and is marked by rapid brain growth during early childhood. Many sufferers are mentally retarded and require lifelong institutional care. But autism has many other faces. The condition, as experts now conceive it, is like high blood pressure—a "spectrum disorder" in which affected people differ from the rest of us only by degrees. The question is, degrees of what? Can autistic tendencies be measured on some scale? If so, is there a clear boundary between normal and abnormal? And is abnormality always a bad thing? What promise does life hold for people like Andrew?

Cambridge University psychologist Simon Baron-Cohen has a thesis that bears on all these questions. In a bold new book called "The Essential Difference," he defines autism as an imbalance between two kinds of intelligence: the kind used to understand people (he calls it "empathizing") and the kind used to understand things ("systemizing"). Though most of us have both abilities, studies suggest that females are better than males at empathizing, while males have a stronger knack for systemizing. By Baron-Cohen's account, autism is just an exaggerated version of the male profile—an extreme fondness for rule-based systems, coupled with an inability to intuit people's feelings and intentions. The truth may not be quite that simple, but the concepts of "E" and "S" offer a powerful new framework for thinking about boys, girls and autism. If Baron-Cohen is right, autism is not just a disease in need of a cure. It's a mental style that people can learn to accommodate. Sometimes it's even a gift.

It's no secret that autism affects boys more than girls. Males account for more than 80 percent of the million-plus Americans with autistic disorders. Are these conditions partly an expression of male thought patterns? Do boys live closer to the autistic spectrum than girls? Not in every case. But when researchers study groups of people—infants, toddlers, teens or adults—an interesting pattern emerges. Newborn girls gaze longer at faces than at mechanical mobiles, while boys show the opposite preference. By the age of 3, girls are more adept than boys at imagining fictional characters' feelings, and by 7 they're better at identifying a faux pas in a story. The disparity is just as striking when adults are asked to interpret facial expressions and tones of voice. Women rule.

Males aren't hopeless, though. They show a lifelong advantage on tests of spatial and mechanical reasoning. In fact they're nearly twice as likely as women to score more than 700 on the SAT math test, and four times as likely to become engineers. Social conditioning may account for some of that gap. It may also help explain the thrill that 2-year-old boys get from trucks, blocks and other mechanical toys. But there has to be more to the story. Consider what happened when psychologists Gerianne Alexander and Melissa Hines tried out six toys on vervet monkeys at UCLA's Non-Human Primate Laboratory. Male monkeys favored the boy toys (a ball and a car). Females spent more time with a doll and a pot. And the gender-neutral toys (a picture book and a stuffed dog) got equal attention from both groups. The findings suggest that sex hormones may sculpt our brains as well as our bodies, priming males and females for different styles of thought—what Baron-Cohen calls a "Type E" style and a "Type S" style.

It's not hard to see how autism fits into this scheme. In its classic form, the condition leaves people virtually devoid of social impulses. Autistic kids have trouble communicating, and games like peekaboo leave them cold. They seem to perceive people as unpredictable objects. Yet they often excel at systemizing. "Even young autistic children love to classify and order things," says Dr. Bryna Siegel of the University of California, San Francisco. "They're interested in categorical information." Siegel recalls a mother's story about taking her autistic son and nonautistic daughters to see "Finding Nemo," a movie about a clown fish who loses his mom and gets separated from his dad. "The little girls wanted to know if Nemo was scared," she says. "The autistic boy wanted to know exactly what clown fish eat."

Autistic people are famous for collecting such facts, and many can recall them with breathtaking precision. Patricia Juhrs, director of a Rockville, Md., group called Community Services for Autistic Adults and Children, has an adult client who has memorized every top-10 song list *Billboard* magazine has published since 1947. Tell him which day you were born, and he'll tell you what was playing on the radio. Even when they lack such savant skills, autistic people often excel at mundane, detail-oriented tasks. "I maintain that we should have autistic people running the scanners at airports," says Catherine Johnson, an author and activist whose two autistic sons amuse themselves by putting together jigsaw puzzles with the picture-side down. "No normal human being can process that much detail."

She's half joking, but studies support her contention. As you'd expect, autistic people score even lower than typical males on tests that involve predicting people's feelings and interpreting their facial expressions. But when challenged to find the triangle embedded in a complex design, or predict the behavior of a rod attached to a lever, they fare as well as normal males, if not better. The same pattern holds when autistic people are polled directly about empathizing ("I can pick up quickly if someone says one thing and means another") and systemizing ("I am fascinated by how machines work"). In a recently published study, Baron-Cohen's team found that mildly autistic adults trailed normal women and men on a 40-item empathy test, but trumped both groups on a systemizing survey. In short, they were more male than the men.

The findings square nicely with Baron-Cohen's model, but the model takes us only so far. As it turns out, autistic people are not just extreme systemizers. They systemize in a distinct and unusual way. When normally developing kids draw a picture of a train, they start with a gestalt, or general idea: a series of long, flat rectangles with wheels underneath. Autistic kids often start with peripheral details and expand them into dazzling 3-D renderings. "They don't do it in a logical order," says Siegel of UCSF. "They do it as you would if you were tracing." Stephen Wiltshire, 29, had never spoken when he started sketching at the age of 5. He still lives with his mother in West London, but he has since achieved world renown for his visionary portraits of buildings and vehicles. "Cadillac, Chevy, Lincoln," he says when asked about his passions. "Sears Tower, the Frick, the Chrysler building." His speech, like his work, is virtually free of generalizations. As a friend once observed, he is "rooted in the literal, the concrete."

Wiltshire may have Type S tastes, but his avoidance of abstractions can't be passed off as a typical Type S tendency. It gets at something more specific, says neuroscientist Laurent Mottron of Montreal's Hopital Riviere-des-Prairies. It reveals a preference for parts over wholes, a tendency to process information one piece at a time instead of filtering it through general categories. Most of us simplify the world to make it more manageable. Whether we're taking in sights, sounds or sentences, our brains ignore countless details to create useful gestalts. Autistic people make generalizations, too ("it's a train," "it's a blender"), but studies suggest they work from the bottom up, attending doggedly to everything their senses take in. That has nothing to do with maleness, but it helps explain various aspects of autism—the encyclopedic memory, the lightning-fast calculation and the extreme sensitivity to sounds, lights and textures. It also ties in neatly with recent studies linking autism to super-fast brain growth during the first years of life. Researchers believe that process may generate more sensory neurons than the brain can integrate into coherent networks.

Baron-Cohen doesn't dispute any of this. The E-S model may not capture all the nuances of autism, he says, but it sheds new light on the narrow interests and repetitive behaviors that people across the autistic spectrum display. "Consider the child who can spend hours watching how a glass bottle rotates in the sunlight but who cannot talk or make eye contact," he says. "The old theories said that this was purposeless repetitive behavior. The new theory says that the child, given his or her IQ, may be doing something intelligent: looking for predictable rules or patterns in the data." In other words, the E-S model may be incomplete but it's still valuable—for it reveals the sanity and dignity of autistic behavior. "People with Asperger's syndrome [a mild form of autism] are like saltwater fish forced to live in fresh water," a patient once explained to Baron-Cohen. "We're fine if you put us into the right environment. But when the person and the environment don't match, we seem disabled."

Some advocates insist that conditions like Asperger's syndrome are not disorders at all, just personality variants that have been misconstrued as defects. They believe that people at the high-functioning end of the autistic spectrum should be spared psychiatric labels. But when the labels are applied without stigma, they can be liberating.

Dave Spicer had never thought of himself as autistic until 1994, when his 8-year-old son, Andrew, got a formal diagnosis and he was diagnosed too. Spicer, then 46, was a computer programmer and system designer, but his social ineptitude had cost him two marriages and blighted his career. He recalls leaving business meetings thinking all had gone well, only to discover that he had annoyed or offended people. "A social situation is like a square dance where the caller is speaking Swahili," he says. "There will be a cue and I won't get it, and I'll stumble into people." Spicer's son is now thriving in a mainstream high school after several years of special education, and Spicer himself has learned to play to his strengths. He has gone back to college. He socializes on his own terms, and doesn't berate himself for being different. "My favorite story about autism is 'The Emperor's New Clothes,'" he says. "The boy didn't understand social norms, but he spoke the truth. I think society needs us."

Gifted geeks aren't the only ones saying that. Juhrs, the social-service organizer, has found that even profoundly autistic adults are often highly employable. "If they're matched properly with work they enjoy," she says, "they can do as well or better than people who aren't disabled." In seeking out jobs for her clients, Juhrs never appeals to employers for charity. She asks if there are jobs they've had trouble filling. As it turns out, the Type S tasks that her people thrive on—inspecting garments, coding inventory, assembling components for the fuses on nuclear submarines—are often the same ones that ordinary people can't stand. "Once our folks get into going to work, they don't want to miss a day," she says. "We have to talk them into holidays."

Tapping these strengths makes obvious sense, but the deficits associated with autism are just as real. Are people like Spicer destined to fail in love and the workplace, or can their social handicaps be conquered? Unlike systemizing, empathy involves snap, intuitive judgments that you can't always make by following a recipe. "Most people learn to interact socially just by observation," says Stephen Shore, a mildly autistic Boston University doctoral student who heads the Asperger's Association of New England. "People on the autistic spectrum regard things as a set of rules. We have to figure them out or be taught." Like Tom Hanks in "Big," Shore thought sleepover the first time a woman invited him to spend the night. But through painstaking study and practice, he has developed a good enough social repertoire to sustain a career and a 13-year marriage.

Was Shore just lucky, or is there a lesson to be drawn from his experience? Can people on the autistic spectrum learn to compensate for their lack of natural empathizing ability? The answer depends on the person and the condition. Siegel estimates that 25 percent of classically autistic children respond to intensive interventions and that 7 percent do well enough to attend mainstream schools and lead normal lives. The response rates are much higher among mildly affected kids, and experts agree that early intervention is the key to success. "The earlier you can get into a treatment program," says Andy Shih of the National Alliance for Autism Research, "the better the prognosis."

The programs go by different names—applied behavioral analysis, discreet trial training, pivotal response treatment—but most of them use simple conditioning exercises to open lines of communication. "With an average child, you can point to something red and ask what color it is," says psychologist Robert Koegel of the University of California, Santa Barbara. "Autistic kids are screaming, trying to get out of it. But what if they love M&Ms? When we ask which one is red, they take a red one. They're highly motivated." Naming colors is simpler than decoding social signals, but they, too, can be mastered by unconventional means. Baron-Cohen's team has developed an interactive computer program that pairs 418 emotions with distinct facial expressions.

Preliminary studies suggest that anyone, autistic or not, can develop a better eye for flattery, boredom or scorn simply by practicing for 10 weeks with these electronic flashcards.

As fate would have it, some of the best natural readers of feelings and faces are themselves profoundly disabled. People with a rare genetic disorder called Williams syndrome are often severely retarded. Yet they're hypersocial, highly verbal and often deeply empathetic. "In some ways," says research psychologist Teresa Doyle of the Salk Institute, "Williams syndrome is almost an opposite of autism." Ten-year-old A. J. Arciniega will never play Bop It Extreme the way Andrew Bacalao does, let alone dismantle a radio. But he shakes hands eagerly when greeted by a *Newsweek* correspondent, and gladly engages in conversation, asking about the visitor's children and their interests. Settling in with a wordless picture book, he pages through the story of a boy and a dog who lose their frog and set out to find him. There is no plot in A. J.'s telling, but his feeling for the characters is irrepressible. "Ron! Ron! Where are you?" he exclaims when the boy is shown calling for his frog. "'Woof! Woof!' the dog moans." Neither Andrew nor A. J. is in for an easy life—as Baron-Cohen might say, things are simpler in the middle of the E-S spectrum. But the world will be richer for both of them.

QUESTIONS

1. Why do some researchers describe autism as an "exaggerated version of the male profile"? Do you think this association is valid?

2. How is the unusually rapid brain growth and overabundance of sensory neurons implicated in the cause of autism?

3. Is it important for children diagnosed with autism to be involved in treatment early on? Why or why not?

8

New Attention to ADHD Genes

Researchers Are Trying to Tease Apart the Genetic and Environmental Contributions to Childhood's Most Common Mental Disorder

Kathryn Brown

"Passionate, deviant, spiteful, and lacking inhibitory volition." That's how one pediatrician, George Frederick Still, described children with symptoms of attention deficit hyperactivity disorder (ADHD). The year was 1902, and Still puzzled over his young patients in *The Lancet*. What was their disorder, exactly—and what caused it?

A century later, scientists would still like to know. As skyrocketing numbers of children are diagnosed with ADHD and prescribed drugs, researchers are falling under increasing pressure to explain the disorder (*Science*, 14 March, p. 1646). Is ADHD the result of faulty brain wiring? Which genes are to blame? And how much does environment matter? Emerging studies, harnessing genome scans and other high-tech tools, promise new insights. But as Judith Rapoport, chief of child psychiatry at the National Institute of Mental Health (NIMH) puts it, "there's been no home run yet."

Like any complex disorder, ADHD is a one-two punch of susceptibility genes and environmental risks. Together they cause severe inattention, hyperactivity, or both, says clinical psychologist Stephen Faraone of Harvard University. "My hope is that once we've discovered those genes, we'll be able to do a prospective study of kids at high versus low genetic risk," Faraone says. "That's when you'll see environmental factors at work." Eventually, he adds, environmental changes could play an important role in treating some ADHD patients.

"New Attention to ADHD Genes," by Kathryn Brown, *Science*, July 11, 2003, p. 160–162.
Copyright © 2003 by the American Association for the Advancement of Science.
Reprinted by permission.

IN THE FAMILY

Since the 1800s, doctors have labeled some children as overwhelmingly distracted or fidgety. Depending on the diagnosis of the day, they suffered from "childhood hyperactivity," "hyperkinetic syndrome" or "minimal brain dysfunction."

In the 1980s, the American Psychiatric Association defined ADHD in the *Diagnostic and Statistical Manual of Mental Disorders* (DSM) for the first time. According to the current, revised DSM definition, a person with ADHD has been severely inattentive (forgetful, careless, distracted, etc.) or hyperactive/impulsive (restless, impatient, aggressive, etc.) for at least 6 months. To qualify as ADHD, those symptoms must emerge before 7 years of age, be maladaptive and inconsistent with developmental level, and impair social or work routines in at least two settings, usually home and school.

According to NIMH, ADHD is the most commonly diagnosed mental disorder in childhood, estimated to affect 3% to 5% of school-age children. The proportion of children diagnosed with ADHD has risen steadily over the past 15 years, but researchers argue over whether this represents a real increase, overdiagnosis, or better recognition of ADHD after years of underdiagnosing the condition.

Skeptics still question whether ADHD is an authentic disorder and not simply a pathological label for normal, if exasperating, childhood behavior. But most scientists who study the condition are convinced. Over the past decade, more than 10 studies of twins in far-flung locations have suggested that ADHD has a strong genetic component. Heritability for ADHD—meaning that if one identical twin has it, the other will, too—ranges from 65% to 90%, comparable to schizophrenia and bipolar disorder, Faraone says.

In fact, researchers know more about ADHD genes than those behind several other complex behavioral disorders, such as Tourette's syndrome, asserts molecular geneticist Cathy Barr of Toronto Western Hospital. "We've made good progress, replicating, studies on several genes," Bart says. "At the very least, this new research contributes to the idea that ADHD is biologically based—that there's something here."

That "something" likely includes the neurotransmitter dopamine. Paradoxically, stimulants, including methylphenidate (Ritalin), calm rather than excite children with ADHD. Researchers have long suspected that such drugs work by indirectly regulating dopamine levels in the brain. Based on that hunch, they are hunting genes that affect dopamine communication, notably a receptor (DRD4), a transporter (DAT), and a protein called synaptosomal-associated protein 25 (SNAP-25) that helps trigger the release of neurotransmitters from nerve cells. Genetic linkage studies of each gene have associated variants with ADHD symptoms. But more research is needed to explain the underlying biochemistry.

Some researchers even suggest that ADHD may be too much of a good thing. Last year in the Proceedings of the National Academy of Sciences, for instance, Robert Moyzis of the University of California, Irvine, and his colleagues reported that one variety of the DRD4 gene associated with ADHD—the so-called seven-repeat allele, or DRD4 7R—appears to have been selected for in human evolution, suggesting that it supported an adaptive trait.

"Kids with this gene version may have inherited faster reaction times or different attention spans, and now we're calling this a disorder," Moyzis says. "Maybe all you need to do is steer those kids into a different educational situation."

One thing seems clear: No matter how these purported ADHD genes affect dopamine, they cannot cause the disorder by themselves. So far, scientists estimate that each gene confers a very low added risk—roughly 1% to 3%—of developing ADHD. How are other neurotransmitters involved? Some scientists are investigating genes that regulate norepinephrine and nicotine levels in the brain. At Washington University in St. Louis, Missouri, for instance, molecular geneticist Richard Todd and his colleagues report that twins with ADHD often share a form of nicotinic acetylcholine receptor alpha 4, although the link is preliminary.

SCANNING THE FUTURE

Meanwhile, a few researchers are betting that critical ADHD genes, contributing far greater risk, remain undiscovered. They've begun using genome scans to randomly hunt for these susceptibility genes. Genome scans compare hundreds of known DNA markers between two siblings sharing the disorder. Any DNA regions with unusually high (more than 50%) similarity between those siblings may contain risk genes.

Susan Smalley, a geneticist at the University of California, Los Angeles, recently led the first genome scans of siblings sharing ADHD. "We're operating on the idea that a couple of genes may add 10% to 25% of ADHD risk," Smalley says. In the May issue of the *American Journal of Human Genetics,* Smalley's group described scanning the genomes of 270 sibling pairs with ADHD. They found hints of ADHD genes on chromosomes 5, 6, 16, and 17.

"What's intriguing is that several of these gene regions overlap with those implicated in autism and dyslexia," Smalley says. She suspects that these disorders may share a neurological glitch that disrupts the brain's "executive function" system—neural networks that govern tasks such as problem-solving, planning, and attention. Faraone calls the study a "very impressive" step toward isolating promising genes.

In the same journal issue, medical geneticist Richard Sinke of the University Medical Center in Utrecht, the Netherlands, and colleagues reported an ADHD genome scan with fewer children. It mostly highlighted different chromosomal regions but overlapped with the site that Smalley's team found on chromosome 5. Now the two teams are analyzing their data together.

Environmental risks, researchers predict, will be even harder to pin down than genes contributing to ADHD. They've begun linking ADHD symptoms to lifestyle factors, from maternal smoking during pregnancy to chronic family conflict. But because such adversities boost the risk of many disorders, the links are hard to interpret.

Still, genes promise an analytical starting point. In the next 10 years, Faraone and others hope to use genetic tests to identify preschoolers at high or low risk of ADHD. Tracking both sets of children, they could look for specific environmental factors that trigger ADHD symptoms. "How do genes work in different environments?" muses Smalley. "How do genes lead to impairment? That's the next step."

QUESTIONS

1. Which neurotransmitter is likely associated with ADHD, and how do stimulant medications effect children with ADHD?
2. Why are environmental factors so much more difficult to tease out than genes in terms of potential causes of ADHD?
3. After reading this article, are you more or less convinced than you were before that ADHD has a biological cause? Why?

9

The New Science
of Dyslexia

*Why Some Children Struggle So Much
With Reading Used to Be a Mystery.
Now Researchers Know What's
Wrong—And What to Do About It*

Christine Gorman

*Byline: Christine Gorman Reported by Paul Cuadros/Chapel Hill, Greg Land/
Atlanta, Sean Scully/Los Angeles and Sora Song/New York*

When Sean Slattery, 17, looks at a page of text, he can see the letters. He can tell you the letters' names. He can even tell you what sounds those letters make. But it often takes a while for the articulate high school student from Simi Valley, Calif., to tell you what words those letters form. "I see a wall," he says. "I see a hurdle I have to get over." Some words are easier for Sean to figure out than others. "I can get longer words, like electricity," he says. "But I have trouble with shorter words, like four or year."

Slattery has dyslexia, a reading disorder that persists despite good schooling and normal or even above-average intelligence. It's a handicap that affects up to 1 in 5 schoolchildren. Yet the exact nature of the problem has eluded doctors, teachers, parents and dyslexics themselves since it was first described more than a century ago. Indeed, it is so hard for skilled readers to imagine what it's like not to be able to effortlessly absorb the printed word that they often suspect the real problem is laziness or obstinacy or a proud parent's inability to recognize that his or her child isn't that smart after all.

The mystery—and perhaps some of the stigma—may finally be starting to lift. The more researchers learn about dyslexia, the more they realize it's a flaw not of character but of biology—specifically, the biology of the brain. No, people with dyslexia are not brain damaged. Brain scans show their cerebrums are perfectly normal, if not extraordinary. Dyslexics, in fact, seem to have a distinct advantage when it comes to thinking outside the box.

But a growing body of scientific evidence suggests there is a glitch in the neurological wiring of dyslexics that makes reading extremely difficult for them. Fortunately, the science also points to new strategies for overcoming the glitch. The most successful programs focus on strengthening the brain's aptitude for linking letters to the sounds they represent. (More later on why that matters.) Some studies suggest that the right kinds of instruction provided early enough may rewire the brain so thoroughly that the neurological glitch disappears entirely.

The new science may even be starting to change public policy. When the U.S. government launched an education initiative in 2001 called No Child Left Behind, its administrators made clear that their funding would go only to reading programs that are based on solid evidence of the sort that has been uncovered in dyslexia research. "In education, the whole idea that there is evidence that some programs are more effective than others is new," says Dr. Sally Shaywitz, a Yale neuroscientist who has written a fascinating new book, *Overcoming Dyslexia* (Alfred A. Knopf; April 2003), that details the latest brain-scan research—much of it done in her lab. "The good news is we really understand the steps of how you become a reader and how you become a skilled reader," she says.

Along the way, a number of myths about dyslexia have been exploded. You may have heard, for example, that it's all about flipping letters, writing them backward, Toys 'R' Us style. Wrong. Practically all children make mirror copies of letters as they learn to write, although dyslexics do it more. You may believe that more boys than girls are dyslexic. Wrong again. Boys are just more likely to get noticed because they often vent their frustration by acting out. You may think that dyslexia can be outgrown. This is perhaps the most damaging myth, because it leads parents to delay seeking the extra instruction needed to keep their children from falling further behind. "The majority of students who get identified with learning disorders get identified between the ages of 11 and 17," says Robert Pasternack, assistant secretary for Special Education and Rehabilitative Services. "And that's too late." They can still learn to read, but it will always be a struggle.

This is not to say that dyslexics can't succeed despite their disability. In fact, dyslexics are overrepresented in the top ranks of artists, scientists and business executives. Perhaps because their brains are wired differently, dyslexics are often skilled problem solvers, coming at solutions from novel or surprising angles and making conceptual leaps that leave tunnel-visioned, step-by-step sequential thinkers in the dust. They talk about being able to see things in 3-D Technicolor or as a multidimensional chess game. It may also be that their early struggle with reading better prepares them for dealing with adversity in a volatile, fast-changing world.

But that struggle can cut both ways. Dyslexics are also overrepresented in the prison population. According to Frank Wood, a professor of neurology at Wake Forest University in Winston-Salem, N.C., new research shows that children with dyslexia are more likely than nondyslexics to drop out of school, withdraw from friends and family or attempt suicide.

The stakes have never been higher. Right now in the U.S. there are almost 3 million students in special-education classes specifically because they can't read. Most of them are probably dyslexic. But there are other slow readers who are simply overlooked—ignored in crowded classrooms or dismissed as discipline problems. Unless corrective action is taken, their self-confidence often crumbles as they see other students progressing. Even worse, their peers may taunt or ostracize them—a situation that Sean Slattery's mother Judy remembers all too well. "Sean cried for four hours every day after kindergarten," she says. "He was so unhappy."

To be sure, researchers still don't understand everything there is to know about learning disabilities. Dyslexia, for one, may consist of several subtypes. "It would be very dangerous to assume that every child with reading problems is uniform and has the same kinds of breakdowns preventing him from learning to read," says Dr. Mel Levine, a pediatrician and author of several influential books about learning disabilities and dyslexia, including *A Mind at a Time*. But whatever the exact nature of the deficit, the search for answers begins with the written word.

When you think about it, that anyone can read at all is something of a miracle. Reading requires your brain to rejigger its visual and speech processors in such a way that artificial markings, such as the letters on a piece of paper, become linked to the sounds they represent. It's not enough simply to hear and understand different words. Your brain has to pull them apart into their constituent sounds, or phonemes. When you see the written word cat, your brain must hear the sounds /k/ . . . /a/ . . . /t/ and associate the result with an animal that purrs.

Unlike speech, which any developmentally intact child will eventually pick up by imitating others who speak, reading must be actively taught. That makes sense from an evolutionary point of view. Linguists believe that the spoken word is 50,000 to 100,000 years old. But the written word—and therefore the possibility of reading—has probably been around for no more than 5,000 years. "That's not long enough for our brains to evolve certain regions for just that purpose," says Guinevere Eden, a professor of pediatrics at Georgetown University in Washington, who also uses brain scans to study reading. "We're probably using a whole network of areas in the brain that were originally designed to do something slightly different." As Eden puts it, the brain is moonlighting—and some of the resulting glitches have yet to be ironed out.

To understand what sorts of glitches we're talking about, it helps to know a little about how the brain works. Researchers have long been aware that the two halves, or hemispheres, of the brain tend to specialize in different tasks. Although the division of labor is not absolute, the left side is particularly adept at processing language while the right is more attuned to analyzing spatial cues. The specialization doesn't stop there. Within each hemisphere, different regions of the brain break down various tasks even further. So reading a sonnet, catching a ball or recognizing a face requires the complex interaction of a number of different regions of the brain.

Most of what neuroscientists know about the brain has come from studying people who were undergoing brain surgery or had suffered brain damage. Clearly, this is not the most convenient way to learn about the brain, especially if you want to know more about what passes for normal. Even highly detailed pictures from the most advanced computer-enhanced X-ray imaging machines could reveal only the organ's basic anatomy, not how the various parts worked together. What researchers needed was a scanner that didn't subject patients to radiation and that showed which parts of the brain are most active in healthy subjects as they perform various intellectual tasks. What was needed was a breakthrough in technology.

That breakthrough came in the 1990s with the development of a technique called functional magnetic resonance imaging (fMRI). Basically, fMRI allows researchers to see which parts of the brain are getting the most blood—and hence are the most active—at any given point in time.

Neuroscientists have used fMRI to identify three areas of the left side of the brain that play key roles in reading. Scientifically, these are known as the left inferior frontal gyrus, the left parieto-temporal area and the left occipito-temporal area. But for our purposes, it's more helpful to think of them as the "phoneme producer," the "word analyzer" and the "automatic detector." We'll describe these regions in the order in which they are activated, but you'll get closer to the truth if you think of them as working simultaneously, like the sections of an orchestra playing a symphony.

Using fMRI, scientists have determined that beginning readers rely most heavily on the phoneme producer and the word analyzer. The first of these helps a person say things—silently or out loud—and does some analysis of the phonemes found in words. The second analyzes words more thoroughly, pulling them apart into their constituent syllables and phonemes and linking the letters to their sounds.

As readers become skilled, something interesting happens: the third section—the automatic detector—becomes more active. Its function is to build a permanent repertoire that enables readers to recognize familiar words on sight. As readers progress, the balance of the symphony shifts and the automatic detector begins to dominate. If all goes well, reading eventually becomes effortless.

In addition to the proper neurological wiring, reading requires good instruction. In a study published in the current issue of *Biological Psychiatry,* Shaywitz and colleagues identified a group of poor readers who were not classically dyslexic, as their phoneme producers, word analyzers and automatic detectors were all active. But the three regions were linked more strongly to the brain's memory processors than to its language centers, as if the children had spent more time memorizing words than understanding them.

The situation is different for children with dyslexia. Brain scans suggest that a glitch in their brain prevents them from easily gaining access to the word analyzer and the automatic detector. In the past year, several fMRI studies have shown that dyslexics tend to compensate for the problem by overactivating the phoneme producer.

Here at last is physical evidence that the central weakness in dyslexia is twofold. First, as many dyslexia experts have long suspected, there is an inherent difficulty in deriving sense from phonemes. Second, because recognizing words doesn't become automatic, reading is slow and labored. This second aspect, the lack of fluency, has for the most part not been widely appreciated outside the research community.

Imagine having to deal with each word you see as if you had never come across it before, and you will start to get the idea. That's exactly what Abbe Winn of Atlanta realized her daughter Kate, now 9, was doing in kindergarten. "I noticed that when her teacher sent home a list of spelling words, she had a real hard time," Abbe says. "We'd get to the word *the* and come back five minutes later, and she had no idea what it was."

So much for what dyslexia is. What many parents would like to know is what can be done about it. Fortunately, the human brain is particularly receptive to instruction. Otherwise practice would never make perfect. Different people respond to different approaches, depending on their personality and the nature of their disability. "The data we have don't show any one program that is head and shoulders above the rest," says Shaywitz. But the most successful programs emphasize the same core elements: practice manipulating phonemes, building vocabulary, increasing comprehension and improving the fluency of reading.

This kind of instruction leaves nothing to chance. "In most schools the emphasis is on children's learning to read sentences," says Gina Callaway, director of the Schenck School in Atlanta, which specializes in teaching dyslexic students using the Orton-Gillingham approach. "Here we have to teach them to recognize sounds, then syllables, then words and sentences. There's lots of practice and repetition." And a fair number of what the kids call tricks, or rules, for reading. (Among the most important and familiar: the magic e at the end of a word that makes a vowel say its name, as in make or cute.) A particularly good route to fluency is to practice reading aloud with a skilled reader who can gently correct mistakes. That way the brain builds up the right associations between words and sounds from the start.

There is no reason to assume that the public school system, despite its myriad problems, isn't up to the task. But it's a sad fact of life, particularly in larger or cash-starved institutions, that many kids fall through the cracks. A parent may have to keep up the pressure on the child's school district. Unfortunately, some have had to sue to get results. In extreme cases, parents can be reimbursed for private schooling, as two unanimous decisions by the Supreme Court, in 1985 and 1993, have made clear. (For help finding the right program for your child, see the accompanying story.)

It helps to tap into a student's interests. For Monique Beltran, 13, of Los Angeles, the turning point came with the computer game Pokemon. "I had to read to get to more levels," she says matter-of-factly. The computer game also showed Monique the value of reading outside of schoolwork, and she is eagerly devouring the latest Harry Potter book.

As you might expect, early intervention gives the best results. Yet for decades most schools wouldn't consider special education for a child until he or she had fallen at least a year behind. That may be changing. Congress is considering legislation that would eliminate the need to show a discrepancy between a child's IQ and his or her achievements before receiving a diagnosis of dyslexia.

Ideally, all children should be screened in kindergarten—to minimize educational delay and preserve self-confidence. How do you know someone has dyslexia before he or she has learned to read? Certain behaviors—like trouble rhyming words—are good clues that something is amiss. Later you may notice that your child is memorizing books rather than reading them. A kindergarten teacher's observation that reading isn't clicking with your son or daughter should be a call to action.

If caught soon enough, can a child's dyslexia be reversed? The evidence looks promising. In her book, Shaywitz reports that brain scans of dyslexic kindergartners and first-graders who have benefited from a year's worth of targeted instruction start to resemble those of children who have never had any difficulty reading.

That doesn't mean older folks need despair. Shaywitz's brain scans of adult dyslexics suggest that they can compensate by tapping into the processing power on their brain's right side. Just don't expect what works for young children to work for adults. "If you're 18 and you're about to graduate and you don't have phonemic awareness, that may not be your top priority," says Chris Schnieders, director of teacher training at the Frostig Center in Pasadena, Calif. "It's a little bit late to start 'Buh is for baby' at that point."

Technology can play a supporting role. Some dyslexics supplement their reading with books on tape. (Indeed, in 1995, the Recording for the Blind organization changed its name to Recording for the Blind and Dyslexic in recognition of that fact.) Because their condition affects the ability to write as well as read, a growing number of dyslexics are turning to voice-recognition software for help in preparing term papers, memos and reports. A couple of small studies have shown that the software can also bolster the ability to read. "We found improvement in word recognition, in reading comprehension and spelling," says Marshall Raskind, director of research at the Frostig Center. He suspects that the ability to say, hear and see words almost simultaneously provides good training for the brain.

There are, alas, no quick fixes. Dyslexic students often have to put many more hours into their course work than naturally skilled readers do. But the results are worth it. In the seventh grade, Sean Slattery was barely reading on a first-grade level. Now, after four years at the Frostig Center, he has nearly caught up to where he should be. In May, on his third try, Slattery passed California's high school exit exam.

That's another thing about dyslexics: they learn to persevere. Now Slattery has his eye on a career as an underwater welder. "There's a lot of reading involved" between the course work and the instruction manuals, he says. "But I'm looking forward to it, actually." The written word is not going to hold him back anymore.

ROLE MODELS

Dyslexia didn't stop these famous men and women from achieving greatness. In some cases it may have fueled their creative fires

TOM CRUISE	Even as Top Gun, he says, he was "a functional illiterate." Now he helps kids learn to read
JAY LENO	Tonight Show host may flub a cue card, but the show goes on
AGATHA CHRISTIE	The Queen of Crime struggled with words and yet wrote nearly 100 books, which have sold 2 billion copies
THOMAS EDISON	The man behind the light bulb and phonograph didn't speak until age 4
WALT DISNEY	He was determined to bring his Technicolor imagination to life
WHOOPI GOLDBERG	A high school dropout who turned her talents into Oscar gold

---

HOW THE BRAIN READS WORDS

Using sophisticated imaging techniques to scan the brains of children and adults, researchers have identified three key regions that the brain uses to analyze the printed word, recognize its constituent sounds and automate the process of reading. Although the process has been broken down into a three-step sequence to make it easier to understand, these areas of the brain actually work simultaneously and in concert, like the sections of an orchestra

SEEING THE WORD

For thousands of years, the ears were the primary route by which language entered the human brain. Reading shifted the input to the eyes, requiring the brain to link written markings to spoken language.

In a normal response . . .

1 The Phoneme Producer Left inferior frontal gyrus

Continued

ANIMAL

This section of the brain helps a person vocalize words—silently or out loud. It also starts to analyze phonemes, the smallest sounds that make up words. Cat, for example, contains three phonemes: /k/, /a/ and /t/. This section is especially active in the brains of beginning readers.

2 The Word Analyzer Left parieto-temporal area

AN I MAL

This section of the brain does a more complete analysis of written words. Here they are pulled apart into their constituent syllables and phonemes, and letters are linked to the appropriate sounds.

3 The Automatic Detector Left occipito-temporal area

ANIMAL AN

The job of this part of the brain is to automate the process of recognizing words. The more the automatic detector is activated, the better it functions. Skilled readers can breeze through print with assembly-line-like speed.

WHAT GOES WRONG

AMINAL

The high-speed assembly line breaks down in children with dyslexia. A neurological glitch prevents their brain from easily gaining access to both the word analyzer and the automatic detector. Dyslexics appear to compensate by leaning more heavily on the phoneme producer as well as by recruiting areas from the right side of the brain (not shown) that process visual clues from, for example, accompanying pictures.

Source: *Overcoming Dyslexia,* by Sally Shaywitz M.D. TIME Graphic by Lon Tweeten; text by Christine Gorman

Boys and Girls Are Equally Likely to Suffer From Dyslexia.
Up to 1 in 5 U.S. Schoolchildren Are Living With Dyslexia.

QUESTIONS

1. What are three myths about dyslexia discussed in the article?

2. How does fMRI work, and why is it an important breakthrough?

3. What components do successful reading programs have?

10

The Multitasking Generation

Claudia Wallis

Published in the April 17, 2006 issue: Setting the Record Straight: TITLE TROUBLE Our March 27 story "The Multitasking Generation" incorrectly stated that Patricia Wallace "directs the Johns Hopkins Center for Talented Youth." The center's executive director is Dr. Lea Ybarra. Wallace's title is senior director, information technology and distance education.

They're e-mailing, IMing and downloading while writing the history essay. What is all that digital juggling doing to kids' brains and their family life?

It's 9:30 p.m., and Stephen and Georgina Cox know exactly where their children are. Well, their bodies, at least. Piers, 14, is holed up in his bedroom—eyes fixed on his computer screen—where he has been logged onto a MySpace chat room and AOL Instant Messenger (IM) for the past three hours. His twin sister, Bronte, is planted in the living room, having commandeered her dad's iMac—as usual. She, too, is busily IMing, while chatting on her cell phone and chipping away at homework.

By all standard space-time calculations, the four members of the family occupy the same three-bedroom home in Van Nuys, Calif., but psychologically each exists in his or her own little universe. Georgina, 51, who works for a display-cabinet maker, is tidying up the living room as Bronte works, not that her daughter notices. Stephen, 49, who juggles jobs as a squash coach, fitness trainer, event planner and head of a cancer charity he founded, has wolfed down his dinner alone in the kitchen, having missed supper with the kids. He, too, typically spends the evening on his cell phone and returning e-mails—when he can nudge Bronte off the computer. "One gets obsessed with one's gadgets," he concedes.

Zooming in on Piers' screen gives a pretty good indication of what's on his hyperkinetic mind. O.K., there's a Google Images window open, where he's chasing down pictures of Keira Knightley. Good ones get added to a snazzy Windows Media Player slide show that serves as his personal e-shrine to the actress. Several IM windows are also open, revealing such penetrating conversations as this one with a MySpace pal:

MySpacer: suuuuuup!!! (Translation: What's up?)

Piers: wat up dude

MySpacer: nmu (Not much. You?)

Piers: same

Naturally, iTunes is open, and Piers is blasting a mix of Queen, AC/DC, classic rock and hip-hop. Somewhere on the screen there's a Word file, in which Piers is writing an essay for English class. "I usually finish my homework at school," he explains to a visitor, "but if not, I pop a book open on my lap in my room, and while the computer is loading, I'll do a problem or write a sentence. Then, while mail is loading, I do more. I get it done a little bit at a time."

Bronte has the same strategy. "You just multitask," she explains. "My parents always tell me I can't do homework while listening to music, but they don't understand that it helps me concentrate." The twins also multitask when hanging with friends, which has its own etiquette. "When I talk to my best friend, Eloy," says Piers, "he'll have one earpiece [of his iPod] in and one out." Says Bronte: "If a friend thinks she's not getting my full attention, I just make it very clear that she is, even though I'm also listening to music."

The Coxes are one of 32 families in the Los Angeles area participating in an intensive, four-year study of modern family life, led by anthropologist Elinor Ochs, director of UCLA's Center on Everyday Lives of Families. While the impact of multitasking gadgets was not her original focus, Ochs found it to be one of the most dramatic areas of change since she conducted a similar study 20 years ago. "I'm not certain how the children can monitor all those things at the same time, but I think it is pretty consequential for the structure of the family relationship," says Ochs, whose work on language, interaction and culture earned her a MacArthur "genius" grant.

One of the things Ochs' team of observers looks at is what happens at the end of the workday when parents and kids reunite—and what doesn't happen, as in the case of the Coxes. "We saw that when the working parent comes through the door, the other spouse and the kids are so absorbed by what they're doing that they don't give the arriving parent the time of day," says Ochs. The returning parent, generally the father, was greeted only about a third of the time, usually with a perfunctory "Hi." "About half the time the kids ignored him or didn't stop what they were doing, multitasking and monitoring their various electronic gadgets," she says. "We also saw how difficult it was for parents to penetrate the child's universe. We have so many videotapes of parents actually backing away, retreating from kids who are absorbed by whatever they're doing."

Human beings have always had the capacity to attend to several things at once. Mothers have done it since the hunter-gatherer era—picking berries while suckling an infant, stirring the pot with one eye on the toddler. Nor is electronic multitasking entirely new: we've been driving while listening to car radios since they became popular in the 1930s. But there is no doubt that the phenomenon has reached a kind of warp speed in the era of Web-enabled computers, when it has become routine to conduct six IM conversations, watch *American Idol* on TV and Google the names of last season's finalists all at once.

That level of multiprocessing and interpersonal connectivity is now so commonplace that it's easy to forget how quickly it came about. Fifteen years ago, most home computers weren't even linked to the Internet. In 1990 the majority of adolescents responding to a survey done by Donald Roberts, a professor of communication at Stanford, said the one medium they couldn't live without was a radio/CD player. How quaint. In a 2004 follow-up, the computer won hands down.

Today 82% of kids are online by the seventh grade, according to the Pew Internet and American Life Project. And what they love about the computer, of course, is that it offers the radio/CD thing and so much more—games, movies, e-mail, IM, Google, MySpace. The big finding of a 2005 survey of Americans ages 8 to 18 by the Kaiser Family Foundation, co-authored by Roberts, is not that kids were spending a larger chunk of time using electronic media—that was holding steady at 6.5 hours a day (could it possibly get any bigger?)—but that they were packing more media exposure into that time: 8.5 hours' worth, thanks to "media multitasking"—listening to iTunes, watching a DVD and IMing friends all at the same time. Increasingly, the media-hungry members of Generation M, as Kaiser dubbed them, don't just sit down to watch a TV show with their friends or family. From a quarter to a third of them, according to the survey, say they simultaneously absorb some other medium "most of the time" while watching TV, listening to music, using the computer or even while reading.

Parents have watched this phenomenon unfold with a mixture of awe and concern. The Coxes, for instance, are bowled over by their children's technical prowess. Piers repairs the family computers and DVD player. Bronte uses digital technology to compose elaborate photo collages and create a documentary of her father's ongoing treatment for cancer. And, says Georgina, "they both make these fancy PowerPoint presentations about what they want for Christmas." But both parents worry about the ways that kids' compulsive screen time is affecting their schoolwork and squeezing out family life. "We rarely have dinner together anymore," frets Stephen. "Everyone is in their own little world, and we don't get out together to have a social life."

Every generation of adults sees new technology—and the social changes it stirs—as a threat to the rightful order of things: Plato warned (correctly) that reading would be the downfall of oral tradition and memory. And every generation of teenagers embraces the freedoms and possibilities wrought by technology in ways that shock the elders: just think about what the automobile did for dating.

As for multitasking devices, social scientists and educators are just beginning to assess their impact, but the researchers already have some strong opinions. The mental habit of dividing one's attention into many small slices has significant implications for the way young people learn, reason, socialize, do creative work and understand the world. Although such habits may prepare kids for today's frenzied workplace, many cognitive scientists are positively alarmed by the trend. "Kids that are instant messaging while doing homework, playing games online and watching TV, I predict, aren't going to do well in the long run," says Jordan Grafman, chief of the cognitive neuroscience section at the National Institute of Neurological Disorders and Stroke (NINDS). Decades of research (not to mention common sense) indicate that the quality of one's output and depth of thought deteriorate as one attends to ever more tasks. Some are concerned about the disappearance of mental downtime to relax and reflect. Roberts notes Stanford students "can't go the few minutes between their 10 o'clock and 11 o'clock classes without talking on their cell phones. It seems to me that there's almost a discomfort with not being stimulated—a kind of 'I can't stand the silence.'"

Gen M's multitasking habits have social and psychological implications as well. If you're IMing four friends while watching *That '70s Show*, it's not the same as sitting on the couch with your buddies or your sisters and watching the show together. Or sharing a family meal across a table. Thousands of years of evolution created human physical communication—facial expressions, body language—that puts broadband to shame in its ability to convey meaning and create bonds. What happens, wonders UCLA's Ochs, as we replace side-by-side and eye-to-eye human connections with quick, disembodied e-exchanges? Those are critical issues not just for social scientists but for parents and teachers trying to understand—and do right by—Generation M.

YOUR BRAIN WHEN IT MULTITASKS

Although many aspects of the networked life remain scientifically uncharted, there's substantial literature on how the brain handles multitasking. And basically, it doesn't. It may seem that a teenage girl is writing an instant message, burning a CD and telling her mother that she's doing homework—all at the same time—but what's really going on is a rapid toggling among tasks rather than simultaneous processing. "You're doing more than one thing, but you're ordering them and deciding which one to do at any one time," explains neuroscientist Grafman.

Then why can we so easily walk down the street while engrossed in a deep conversation? Why can we chop onions while watching *Jeopardy*? "We, along with quite a few others, have been focused on exactly this question," says Hal Pashler, psychology professor at the University of California at San Diego. It turns out that very automatic actions or what researchers call "highly practiced skills," like walking or chopping an onion, can be easily done while thinking about other things, although the decision to add an extra onion to a recipe or change the direction in which you're walking is another matter. "It seems that action planning—figuring out what I want to say in response to a person's question or which way I want to steer the car—is usually, perhaps invariably, performed sequentially" or one task at a time, says Pashler. On the other hand, producing the actions you've decided on—moving your hand on the steering wheel, speaking the words you've formulated—can be performed "in parallel with planning some other action." Similarly, many aspects of perception—looking, listening, touching—can be performed in parallel with action planning and with movement.

The switching of attention from one task to another, the toggling action, occurs in a region right behind the forehead called Brodmann's Area 10 in the brain's anterior prefrontal cortex, according to a functional magnetic resonance imaging (fMRI) study by Grafman's team. Brodmann's Area 10 is part of the frontal lobes, which "are important for maintaining long-term goals and achieving them," Grafman explains. "The most anterior part allows you to leave something when it's incomplete and return to the same place and continue from there." This gives us a "form of multitasking," he says, though it's actually sequential processing. Because the prefrontal cortex is one of the last regions of the brain to mature and one of the first to decline with aging, young children do not multitask well, and neither do most adults over 60. New fMRI studies at Toronto's Rotman Research Institute suggest that as we get older, we have more trouble "turning down background thoughts when turning to a new task," says Rotman senior scientist and assistant director Cheryl Grady. "Younger adults are better at tuning out stuff when they want to," says Grady. "I'm in my 50s, and I know that I can't work and listen to music with lyrics; it was easier when I was younger."

But the ability to multiprocess has its limits, even among young adults. When people try to perform two or more related tasks either at the same time or alternating rapidly between them, errors go way up, and it takes far longer—often double the time or more—to get the jobs done than if they were done sequentially, says David E. Meyer, director of the Brain, Cognition and Action Laboratory at the University of Michigan: "The toll in terms of slowdown is extremely large—amazingly so." Meyer frequently tests Gen M students in his lab, and he sees no exception for them, despite their "mystique" as master multitaskers. "The bottom line is that you can't simultaneously be thinking about your tax return and reading an essay, just as you can't talk to yourself about two things at once," he says. "If a teenager is trying to have a conversation on an e-mail chat line while doing algebra, she'll suffer a decrease in efficiency, compared to if she just thought about algebra until she was done. People may think otherwise, but it's a myth. With such complicated tasks [you] will never, ever be able to overcome the inherent limitations in the brain for processing information during multitasking. It just can't be, any more than the best of all humans will ever be able to run a one-minute mile."

Other research shows the relationship between stimulation and performance forms a bell curve: a little stimulation—whether it's coffee or a blaring soundtrack—can boost performance, but too much is stressful and causes a fall-off. In addition, the brain needs rest and recovery time to consolidate thoughts and memories. Teenagers who fill every quiet moment with a phone call or some kind of e-stimulation may not be getting that needed reprieve. Habitual multitasking may condition their brain to an overexcited state, making it difficult to focus even when they want to. "People lose the skill and the will to maintain concentration, and they get mental antsyness," says Meyer.

IS THIS ANY WAY TO LEARN?

Longtime professors at universities around the U.S. have noticed that Gen M kids arrive on campus with a different set of cognitive skills and habits than past generations. In lecture halls with wireless Internet access—now more than 40% of college classrooms, according to the Campus Computing Project—the compulsion to multitask can get out of hand. "People are going to lectures by some of the greatest minds, and they are doing their mail," says Sherry Turkle, professor of the social studies of science and technology at M.I.T. In her class, says Turkle, "I tell them this is not a place for e-mail, it's not a place to do online searches and not a place to set up IRC [Internet relay chat] channels in which to comment on the class. It's not going to help if there are parallel discussions about how boring it is. You've got to get people to participate in the world as it is."

Such concerns have, in fact, led a number of schools, including the M.B.A. programs at UCLA and the University of Virginia, to look into blocking Internet access during lectures. "I tell my students not to treat me like TV," says University of Wisconsin professor Aaron Brower, who has been teaching social work for 20 years. "They have to think of me like a real person talking. I want to have them thinking about things we're talking about."

On the positive side, Gen M students tend to be extraordinarily good at finding and manipulating information. And presumably because modern childhood tilts toward visual rather than print media, they are especially skilled at analyzing visual data and images, observes Claudia Koonz, professor of history at Duke University. A growing number of college professors are using film, audio clips and PowerPoint presentations to play to their students' strengths and capture their evanescent attention. It's a powerful way to teach history, says Koonz. "I love bringing media into the classroom, to be able to go to the website for Edward R. Murrow and hear his voice as he walked with the liberators of Buchenwald." Another adjustment to teaching Generation M: professors are assigning fewer full-length books and more excerpts and articles. (Koonz, however, was stunned when a student matter-of-factly informed her, "We don't read whole books anymore," after Koonz had assigned a 350-page volume. "And this is Duke!" she says.)

Many students make brilliant use of media in their work, embedding audio files and video clips in their presentations, but the habit of grazing among many data streams leaves telltale signs in their writing, according to some educators. "The breadth of their knowledge and their ability to find answers has just burgeoned," says Roberts of his students at Stanford, "but my impression is that their ability to write clear, focused and extended narratives has eroded somewhat." Says Koonz: "What I find is paragraphs that make sense internally, but don't necessarily follow a line of argument."

Koonz and Turkle believe that today's students are less tolerant of ambiguity than the students they taught in the past. "They demand clarity," says Koonz. They want identifiable good guys and bad guys, which she finds problematic in teaching complex topics like Hutu-Tutsi history in Rwanda. She also thinks there are political implications: "Their belief in the simple answer, put together in a visual way, is, I think, dangerous." Koonz thinks this aversion to complexity is directly related to multitasking: "It's as if they have too many windows open on their hard drive. In order to have a taste for sifting through different layers of truth, you have to stay with a topic and pursue it deeply, rather than go across the surface with your toolbar." She tries to encourage her students to find a quiet spot on campus to just think, cell phone off, laptop packed away.

GOT 2 GO. TXT ME L8ER

But turning down the noise isn't easy. By the time many kids get to college, their devices have become extensions of themselves, indispensable social accessories. "The minute the bell rings at most big public high schools, the first thing most kids do is reach into their bag and pick up their cell phone," observes Denise Clark Pope, lecturer at the Stanford School of Education, "never mind that the person [they're contacting] could be right down the hall."

Parents are mystified by this obsession with e-communication—particularly among younger adolescents who often can't wait to share the most mundane details of life. Dominique Jones, 12, of Los Angeles, likes to IM her friends before school to find out what they plan to wear. "You'll get IMs back that say things like 'Oh, my God, I'm wearing the same shoes!' After school we talk about what happened that day, what outfits we want to wear the next day."

Turkle, author of the recently reissued *The Second Self: Computers and the Human Spirit,* has an explanation for this breathless exchange of inanities. "There's an extraordinary fit between the medium and the moment, a heady, giddy fit in terms of social needs." The online environment, she points out, "is less risky if you are lonely and afraid of intimacy, which is almost a definition of adolescence. Things get too hot, you log off, while in real time and space, you have consequences." Teen venues like MySpace, Xanga and Facebook—and the ways kids can personalize their IM personas—meet another teen need: the desire to experiment with identity. By changing their picture, their "away" message, their icon or list of favorite bands, kids can cycle through different personalities. "Online life is like an identity workshop," says Turkle, "and that's the job of adolescents—to experiment with identity."

All that is probably healthy, provided that parents set limits on where their kids can venture online, teach them to exercise caution and regulate how much time they can spend with electronics in general. The problem is that most parents don't. According to the Kaiser survey, only 23% of seventh- to 12th-graders say their family has rules about computer activity; just 17% say they have restrictions on video-game time.

In the absence of rules, it's all too easy for kids to wander into unwholesome neighborhoods on the Net and get caught up in the compulsive behavior that psychiatrist Edward Hallowell dubs "screen-sucking" in his new book, *CrazyBusy.* Patricia Wallace, a techno-psychologist who directs the Johns Hopkins Center for Talented Youth program, believes part of the allure of e-mail—for adults as well as teens—is similar to that of a slot machine. "You have intermittent, variable reinforcement," she explains. "You are not sure you are going to get a reward every time or how often you will, so you keep pulling that handle. Why else do people get up in the middle of the night to check their e-mail?"

GETTING THEM TO LOG OFF

Many educators and psychologists say parents need to actively ensure that their teenagers break free of compulsive engagement with screens and spend time in the physical company of human beings—a growing challenge not just because technology offers such a handy alternative but because so many kids lead highly scheduled lives that leave little time for old-fashioned socializing and family meals. Indeed, many teenagers and college students say overcommitted schedules drive much of their multitasking.

Just as important is for parents and educators to teach kids, preferably by example, that it's valuable, even essential, to occasionally slow down, unplug and take time to think about something for a while. David Levy, a professor at the University of Washington Information School, has found, to his surprise,

that his most technophilic undergraduates—those majoring in "informatics"—
are genuinely concerned about getting lost in the multitasking blur. In an in-
formal poll of 60 students last semester, he says, the majority expressed concerns
about how plugged-in they were and "the way it takes them away from other
activities, including exercise, meals and sleep." Levy's students talked about dif-
ficulties concentrating and their efforts to break away, get into the outdoors
and inside their head. "Although it wasn't a scientific survey," he says, "it was
the first evidence I had that people in this age group are reflecting on these
questions."

For all the handwringing about Generation M, technology is not really
the problem. "The problem," says Hallowell, "is what you are not doing if the
electronic moment grows too large"—too large for the teenager and too large
for those parents who are equally tethered to their gadgets. In that case, says
Hallowell, "you are not having family dinner, you are not having conversations, you are not debating whether to go out with a boy who wants to have
sex on the first date, you are not going on a family ski trip or taking time just
to veg. It's not so much that the video game is going to rot your brain, it's
what you are not doing that's going to rot your life."

Generation M has a lot to teach parents and teachers about what new technology can do. But it's up to grownups to show them what it can't do, and
that there's life beyond the screen.

TIPS FOR PARENTS

Dr. Edward Hallowell, a psychiatrist and author of the new book
*CrazyBusy: Overstretched, Overbooked and About to Snap—Strategies for
Coping in a World Gone ADD,* offers some guidelines for parents of
Generation M:

DO see for yourself what it's all about. Get on IM. Download an
MP3 music file. Play a video game. Create a MySpace account. Let your
kids be your guide, but talk to them about how to use these technologies safely and wisely.

DON'T be a disapproving elder. Every older generation believes the
younger generation is on the road to perdition. Your kids need your cu-
riosity and involvement, not pious, uninformed pronouncements.

DO set limits, monitor content and teach "techno-manners" for
everyone: No cell phones at the dinner table. No playing video games
while someone is trying to talk to you. No ignoring Mom and Dad
when they come home because you are glued to a screen.

DON'T be a screen-sucker. Monitor your own online behavior and
television viewing. A major reason for the disappearance of the human
moment in families is the parents'—not just the kids'—addiction to
screens.

Continued

DO look for the good. Search for what's positive and innovative in the ways in which your children are using and adapting to the new technology. Try to imagine how it could be used to enhance relationships and learning.

DON'T let technology steal your kids from you. Enjoy your children. Cherish the face-to-face conversations, the shared laughter, the dinner with all the family, the bedtime story, the car ride without the iPod, video game or fold-down DVD.

DO take time to hang out with your kids. Do mundane, nontechnological things: wash the car together, play Ping-Pong, debate politics, take them out for ice cream (no cell phones or iPods allowed). Spend time together with ears and eyes available for them.

HOW THE BRAIN TOGGLES

Imaging studies have begun to reveal the anatomy of multitasking. Young adults have some advantages.

THE MEDIAL PARIETAL LOBES

These areas are active when you are not focused on a task; they are considered default regions. When turning to a task, young adults do better than older adults in quieting the activity of the default regions. That may explain why older adults are more distracted by background thoughts ("Did I return that call?").

BRODMANN'S AREA 10

This section of the anterior prefrontal cortex acts as the switching station for multitasking. fMRI studies show increased blood flow to that region when one turns from one task to another and when one resumes the first task. The prefrontal cortex is much more highly developed in humans than in lower primates. It is one of the last to mature in adolescence and one of the first to decline with aging. Young children and people over 60 tend to be less adept at multitasking than young adults.

"[Students] can't go a few minutes without talking on their cell phones. There's almost a discomfort with not being stimulated—a kind of 'I can't stand the silence.'"
—DONALD ROBERTS, Stanford professor

QUESTIONS

1. Where is Brodmann's Area 10 located in the brain? Explain the role of Brodmann's Area 10 in multitasking.

2. What happens to the number of errors and the time involved when students multitask rather than perform tasks sequentially?

3. What are Gen M students extraordinarily good at?

4. What is "The Second Self"? Why are youth likely to "toggle" to the second self?

5. What are the possible social developmental consequences when children spend too much time in the online environment?

11

The Adolescent Brain

Beyond Raging Hormones

President and Fellows of Harvard College

Neuroscience research is suggesting some reasons why teenagers are that way. In every generation, it seems, the same lament goes forth from the parents of adolescents: "What's the matter with kids today?" Why are they so often confused, annoying, demanding, moody, defiant, reckless? Accidental deaths, homicides, and binge drinking spike in the teenage years. It's the time of life when psychosis, eating disorders, and addictions are most likely to take hold. Surveys show that everyday unhappiness also reaches its peak in late adolescence.

Plenty of explanations for teenage turmoil are available. Adolescents need to assert their independence and explore their limits, taking risks, breaking rules, and rebelling against their parents while still relying on them for support and protection. ("What's the matter with the older generation?") They have to cope with disconcerting new sexual impulses and romantic feelings. Cultural change heightens incompatibility between the generations. Now scientific research is suggesting a new reason for the clashes between teenagers and their environment. Unsettled moods and unsettling behavior may be rooted in uneven brain development.

It's not a question of intellectual maturity. Most studies show that abstract reasoning, memory, and the formal capacity for planning are fully developed by age 15 or 16. If teenagers are asked hypothetical questions about risk and reward, they usually give the same answers as adults. But the emotional state in which they answer questionnaires is not necessarily the one in which they make important choices. In real life, adolescents, compared to adults, find it more difficult to interrupt an action under way (stop speeding); to think before acting (learn how deep the water is before you dive); and even to choose between safer and riskier alternatives. It is easy for them to say that they would not get into a car with a drunk driver, but more difficult to turn down the invitation in practice. Adolescents' judgment can be overwhelmed by the urge for new experiences, thrill-seeking, and sexual and aggressive impulses. They sometimes seem driven to seek experiences that produce strong feelings and sensations.

Resisting social pressure is also more difficult for teenagers. Much of their troubling behavior, from gang violence to reckless driving and drinking, occurs in groups and because of group pressure. In a psychological experiment, adolescents and adults took a driving simulation test that allowed them to win a reward by running a yellow light and stopping before they hit a wall. Adolescents, but not adults, were more likely to take extra chances when friends were watching.

Another revealing psychological experiment is the Iowa gambling task. Subjects can choose from one of two decks of cards in the hope of picking a card that provides a reward. The "good" deck contains many cards that provide some reward; the "bad" one, many cards that provide nothing and insufficient compensation in the form of a few that hold a jackpot. The choices of adults correspond fairly well to their tested reasoning capacity. In adolescence, the correlation is much weaker.

Evidence is appearing that these differences have a definite basis in brain structure and functioning. Recent research has shown that human brain circuitry is not mature until the early 20s (some would add, "if ever"). Among the last connections to be fully established are the links between the prefrontal cortex, seat of judgment and problem-solving, and the emotional centers in the limbic system, especially the amygdala. These links are critical for emotional learning and high-level self-regulation.

Beginning at puberty, the brain is reshaped. Neurons (gray matter) and synapses (junctions between neurons) proliferate in the cerebral cortex and are then gradually pruned throughout adolescence. Eventually, more than 40% of all synapses are eliminated, largely in the frontal lobes. Meanwhile, the white insulating coat of myelin on the axons that carry signals between nerve cells continues to accumulate, gradually improving the precision and efficiency of neuronal communication—a process not completed until the early 20s. The corpus callosum, which connects the right and left hemispheres of the brain, consists mostly of this white matter.

Another circuit still under construction in adolescence links the prefrontal cortex to the midbrain reward system, where addictive drugs and romantic love exert their powers. Most addictions get their start in adolescence, and there is evidence that adolescent and adult brains respond differently to drugs. In both human beings and laboratory rats, studies have found that adolescents become addicted to nicotine faster and at lower doses. Functional brain scans also suggest that teenagers and adults process reward stimuli differently; the adolescents are hypersensitive to the value of novel experiences.

Hormonal changes are at work, too. The adolescent brain pours out adrenal stress hormones, sex hormones, and growth hormone, which in turn influence brain development. The production of testosterone increases

10 times in adolescent boys. Sex hormones act in the limbic system and in the raphe nucleus, source of the neurotransmitter serotonin, which is important for the regulation of arousal and mood. The hormonally regulated 24-hour clocks change their settings during adolescence, keeping high school and college students awake far into the night and making it difficult to rise for morning classes.

As long as the brain is still in formation, things can go wrong in many ways, and some of them involve the onset of psychiatric disorders. Stress can retard the growth of the hippocampus, which consolidates memories. According to some theories, the pruning of gray matter or the thickening of the myelin coat in late adolescence allows the early symptoms of schizophrenia to emerge.

At least one important social policy conclusion may have been drawn in part from the neuroscience research on the adolescent brain. In 2005, the Supreme Court, affirming a Missouri high court decision, declared by a vote of 5-4 that the execution of 16- and 17-year-olds is unconstitutionally cruel and unusual punishment. The minimum age for capital punishment is now the same as the minimum age for voting and serving on juries. In writing their decision, the justices referred to evolving standards of decency, practices in other countries, the immaturity of adolescents, and their greater potential for change. They did not specifically mention brain research, but they had the opportunity to read friend-of-the-court briefs citing this research that were submitted by the American Bar Association, American Academy of Child and Adolescent Psychiatry, and American Psychiatric Association, among others.

Some critics, even if they welcome the Supreme Court decision for other reasons, have complained that this research stereotypes adolescents and provides a biological rationalization for irresponsible behavior. Animal experiments have limited value because laboratory animals do not undergo a lengthy human childhood. And human brain development does not unfold automatically and uniformly. There is much individual variation that reflects experience as well as genetic programming. The problems of teenagers are not all in their brains but have many causes, social and individual, genetic and environmental. At present and probably for a long time, researchers will be getting better information on the mental and emotional development of adolescents from interviews, observations, and behavioral tests than from brain scans.

But neuroscience research is becoming more sophisticated. There are already long-term studies in which people undergo frequent periodic brain scans over the course of their lives. The results are being used to investigate the effects of behavioral and cognitive therapies on attention deficit disorder and reading deficiencies in adolescents. Scientists are also looking at typical adolescent brain development to provide clues to the ways in which things go wrong. Some day, this research may provide results that will influence treatments for psychiatric disorders and other problems in adolescence.

REFERENCES

Giedd JN. "Structural Magnetic Resonance Imaging of the Adolescent Brain," *Annals of the New York Academy of Sciences* (June 2004): Vol. 1021, pp. 77–85.

Kelley AE, et al. "Risk Taking and Novelty Seeking in Adolescence," *Annals of the New York Academy of Sciences* (June 2004): Vol. 1021, pp. 27–32.

Rosso IM, et al. "Cognitive and Emotional Components of Frontal Lobe Functioning in Childhood and Adolescence," *Annals of the New York Academy of Sciences* (June 2004): Vol. 1021, pp. 355–62.

Spessot AL, et al. "Neuroimaging of Developmental Psychopathologies: The Importance of Self-Regulatory and Neural Plastic Processes in Adolescence," *Annals of the New York Academy of Sciences* (June 2004): Vol. 1021, pp. 86–104.

Steinberg L. "Cognitive and Affective Development in Adolescence," *Trends in Cognitive Science* (February 2005): Vol. 9, No. 2, pp. 68–75.

For more references, please see www.health.harvard.edu/mentalextra.

QUESTIONS

1. What is the new theory behind adolescent turmoil?

2. Human brain circuiting is probably not mature until the early 20's. What are the last connections to be made?

3. How has the research discussed in this article contributed to social policy changes?

12

Internet Gives Teenage Bullies Weapons to Wound From Afar

Amy Harmon

The fight started at school, when some eighth-grade girls stole a pencil case filled with makeup that belonged to a new classmate, Amanda Marcuson, and she reported them.

But it did not end there. As soon as Amanda got home, the instant messages started popping up on her computer screen. She was a tattletale and a liar, they said. Shaken, she typed back, "You stole my stuff!" She was a "stuck-up bitch," came the instant response in the box on the screen, followed by a series of increasingly ugly epithets.

That evening, Amanda's mother tore her away from the computer to go to a basketball game with her family. But the barrage of electronic insults did not stop. Like a lot of other teenagers, Amanda has her Internet messages automatically forwarded to her cellphone, and by the end of the game she had received 50—the limit of its capacity.

"It seems like people can say a lot worse things to someone online than when they're actually talking to them," said Amanda, 14, of Birmingham, Mich., who transferred to the school last year. The girls never said another word to her in person, she said.

The episode reflects one of many ways that the technology lubricating the social lives of teenagers is amplifying standard adolescent cruelty. No longer confined to school grounds or daytime hours, "cyberbullies" are pursuing their quarries into their own bedrooms. Tools like e-mail messages and Web logs enable the harassment to be both less obvious to adults and more publicly humiliating, as gossip, put-downs and embarrassing pictures are circulated among a wide audience of peers with a few clicks.

The technology, which allows its users to inflict pain without being forced to see its effect, also seems to incite a deeper level of meanness. Psychologists say the distance between bully and victim on the Internet is leading to an unprecedented—and often unintentional—degree of brutality, especially when combined with a typical adolescent's lack of impulse control and underdeveloped empathy skills.

"We're always talking about protecting kids on the Internet from adults and bad people," said Parry Aftab, executive director of WiredSafety.org, a nonprofit group that has been fielding a growing number of calls from parents and school administrators worried about bullying. "We forget that we sometimes need to protect kids from kids."

For many teenagers, online harassment has become a part of everyday life. But schools, which tend to focus on problems that arise on their property, and parents, who tend to assume that their children know better than they do when it comes to computers, have long overlooked it. Only recently has it become pervasive enough that even the adults have started paying attention.

Like many other guidance counselors, Susan Yuratovac, a school psychologist at Hilltop Elementary School in Beachwood, Ohio, has for years worked with a wide spectrum of teenage aggression, including physical bullying and sexual harassment. This summer, Ms. Yuratovac said, she is devising a new curriculum to address the shift to electronic taunting.

"I have kids coming into school upset daily because of what happened on the Internet the night before," Ms. Yuratovac said. "'We were online last night and somebody said I was fat,' or 'They asked me why I wear the same pair of jeans every day,' or 'They say I have Wal-Mart clothes.'"

Recently, Ms. Yuratovac intervened when a 12-year-old girl showed her an instant message exchange in which a boy in her class wrote, "My brother says you have really good boobs." Boys make many more explicit sexual comments online than off, counselors say.

"I don't think the girl is fearful the boy is going to accost her, but I do think she is embarrassed," Ms. Yuratovac said. "They know it's mean, it's risky, it's nasty. I worry what it does to them inside. It's the kind of thing you carry with you for a lot of years."

The new weapons in the teenage arsenal of social cruelty include stealing each others' screen names and sending inflammatory messages to friends or crush-objects, forwarding private material to people for whom it was never intended and anonymously posting derogatory comments about fellow students on Web journals called blogs.

"Everyone hates you," read an anonymous comment directed toward a girl who had signed her name to a post about exams on a blog run by middle-school students at the Maret School in Washington, D.C., last term.

"They would talk about one girl in particular who had an acne problem, calling her pimpleface and things like that which was really mean," one Maret student said. "That stuck with me because I've had acne, too."

One of the girls who started the blog said she and her friends had deleted all the posts because so many people—including some parents—began to complain.

"I didn't see why they cared so much," said the girl, who preferred not to be identified. "It's obviously not as serious as it seems if no one's coming up to you and saying it."

Rosalind Wiseman, whose book "Queen Bees and Wannabes," was the basis for the recent movie "Mean Girls," said that online bullying had a particular appeal for girls, who specialize in emotional rather than physical harassment and strive to avoid direct confrontation. But boys do their fair share as well, often using modern methods to betray the trust of adolescent girls.

For instance, last spring, when an eighth-grade girl at Horace Mann School in the Riverdale section of the Bronx, sent a digital video of herself masturbating to a male classmate on whom she had a crush, it quickly appeared on a file-sharing network that teenagers use to trade music. Hundreds of New York private school students saw the video, in which the girl's face was clearly visible, and it was available to a worldwide audience of millions.

Students would go online at school while the girl was there and watch it, said one student from another school, who declined to be named. Horace Mann officials did not reply to requests for comment this week, but the student newspaper reported at the time that the school had set up out-of-school counseling for the students directly involved and held assemblies to discuss issues of sexuality and communication.

The incident is not an isolated one. In June, a video showing two Scarsdale High School freshman girls in a sexual encounter, apparently taking direction from boys in the background, prompted an investigation by the Westchester County district attorney's office when a parent reported that students were sending it to each other by e-mail. A nude picture of a 15-year-old in Wycoff, N.J., taken with a camera phone, is still circulating after she sent it by e-mail to her boyfriend and he forwarded it to his friends, other students said.

Online lists rating a school's girls as "hottest," "ugliest" or "most boring" are common. One that surfaced at Horace Greeley High School in Chappaqua, N.Y., a few years ago, listed names, phone numbers and what were said to be the sexual exploits of dozens of girls.

But girls are not the only victims of Internet-fueled gossip. A seventh grader at Nightingale-Bamford School in Manhattan said she had recently seen an online video a boy had made of himself singing a song to a girl he liked, who promptly posted it all over the Internet. "I feel really bad for the guy," she said.

To a large degree, psychologists say, teenagers are being tripped up by the same property of the Internet that has compelled many adults to fire off an e-mail message they later regret: the ability to press "send" and watch it disappear makes it seem less real.

"It isn't quite the same as taking a dirty picture of your girlfriend and showing it to everyone in the school when you're standing there holding the picture," said Sherry Turkle, a psychologist at the Massachusetts Institute of Technology and author of "Life on the Screen." "There's something about the medium that has a coarsening effect."

But a growing number of teenagers are learning the hard way that words sent into cyberspace can have more severe consequences than a telephone conversation or a whispered confidence. As ephemeral as they seem, instant messages (better known as I.M.'s) form a written record often wielded as a potent weapon for adolescent betrayal and torment.

A sophomore girl at Fieldston High School in the Bronx, for instance, agreed not to return this fall after a racist comment she wrote in an instant message to a friend about a boy who had spurned her ignited controversy last spring. The friend forwarded the message to the boy, and copies were distributed around the school the next day, people familiar with the situation said.

Fieldston High officials declined to comment, as did the girl and her parents, who requested that her name be withheld to protect her at her new school. But several parents criticized the school administration for pressuring the girl to leave rather than using the incident as a means to teach a lesson about racist speech—and the pitfalls of instant messaging.

"When you say things over the Internet, it feels like you are spewing into your diary," said Sandra Pirie Carson, the parent of a Fieldston graduate and a lawyer who offered to mediate between the school and the girl's family. "If she had said those offensive things to her friend on the phone, I have a feeling the friend wouldn't have called him and repeated what she said, and even if she had, I doubt it would have had the same effect."

Many schools, ill-equipped to handle these new situations, are holding assemblies to talk about them and experts in traditional bullying are scrambling to develop strategies to prevent them.

"It's so nebulous; it's not happening in the lunchroom, it's not happening on the school bus, yet it can spread so quickly," said Mary Worthington, the elementary education coordinator for Network of Victim Assistance, a counseling organization in Bucks County, Pa. "Over the last year when I've been out in schools to do our regular bullying program the counselors will say, 'Can you talk about e-mails or I.M.'s?'"

For parents of several students at the Gillispie School in San Diego, such strategies were to be developed on the fly when online threats between their children and those at another school turned into a more classic form of bullying.

About 30 students from Muirlands School showed up at Gillispie one afternoon last spring, carrying skateboards over their heads and calling out the screen name of one of the boys with whom they had been chatting online.

Kim Penney, the mother of one of the Gillispie boys, said she had since re-moved the Internet cable from the computer in her son's room and insisted that he hold online conversations only where she could see them.

"It was frightening to see the physical manifestation of this back and forth on I.M.," Ms. Penney said. "I just never thought of it as such a big deal."

QUESTIONS

1. What is a "cyberbully"? Why are they able to be more cruel than when bullying in person?
2. Why does this type of bullying appear to appeal to girls in particular?
3. Why is it so difficult to intervene with cyberbullying?

13

Fighting Anorexia: No One to Blame

Peg Tyre

The age of their youngest patients has slipped to 9 years old, and doctors have begun to research the roots of this disease. Anorexia is probably hard-wired, the new thinking goes, and the best treatment is a family affair.

Byline: Peg Tyre (With Karen Springen, Ellise Pierce, Joan Raymond and Dirk Johnson)

Emily Krudys can pinpoint the moment her life fell apart. It was a fall afternoon in the Virginia suburbs, and she was watching her daughter Katherine perform in the school play. Katherine had always been a happy girl, a slim beauty with a megawatt smile, but recently, her mother noticed, she'd been losing weight. "She's battling a virus," Emily kept on telling herself, but there, in the darkened auditorium, she could no longer deny the truth. Under the floodlights, Katherine looked frail, hollow-eyed and gaunt. At that moment, Emily had to admit to herself that her daughter had a serious eating disorder. Katherine was 10 years old.

Who could help their daughter get better? It was a question Emily and her husband, Mark, would ask themselves repeatedly over the next five weeks, growing increasingly frantic as Katherine's weight slid from 48 to 45 pounds. In the weeks after the school play, Katherine put herself on a brutal starvation diet, and no one—not the school psychologist, the private therapist, the family pediatrician or the high-powered internist—could stop her. Emily and Mark tried everything. They were firm. Then they begged their daughter to eat. Then they bribed her. We'll buy you a pony, they told her. But nothing worked. At dinnertime, Katherine ate portions that could be measured in tablespoons. "When I demanded that she eat some food—any food—she'd just shut down," Emily recalls. By Christmas, the girl was so weak she could barely leave the couch. A few days after New Year's, Emily bundled her eldest child into the car and rushed her to the emergency room, where she was immediately put on IV. Home again the following week, Katherine resumed her death march. It took one more hospitalization for the Krudyses to finally make the decision they now believe saved their daughter's life. Last February, they enrolled her in a residential clinic halfway across the country in Omaha, Neb.—one of the few facilities nationwide that specialize in young children with eating disorders. Emily still blames herself for not acting sooner. "It was right in front of me," she says, "but I just didn't realize that children could get an eating disorder this young."

Most parents would forgive Emily Krudys for not believing her own eyes. Anorexia nervosa, a mental illness defined by an obsession with food and acute anxiety over gaining weight, has long been thought to strike teens and young women on the verge of growing up—not kids performing in the fourth-grade production of "The Pig's Picnic." But recently researchers, clinicians and mental-health specialists say they're seeing the age of their youngest anorexia patients decline to 9 from 13. Administrators at Arizona's Remuda Ranch, a residential treatment program for anorexics, received so many calls from parents of young children that last year, they launched a program for kids 13 years old and under; so far, they've treated 69 of them. Six months ago the eating-disorder program at Penn State began to treat the youngest ones, too—20 of them so far, some as young as 8. Elementary schools in Boston, Manhattan and Los Angeles are holding seminars for parents to help them identify eating disorders in their kids, and the parents, who have watched Mary-Kate Olsen morph from a child star into a rail-thin young woman, are all too ready to listen.

At a National Institute of Mental Health conference last spring, anorexia's youngest victims were a small part of the official agenda—but they were the only thing anyone talked about in the hallways, says David S. Rosen, a clinical faculty member at the University of Michigan and an eating-disorder specialist. Seven years ago "the idea of seeing a 9- or 10-year-old anorexic would have been shocking and prompted frantic calls to my colleagues. Now we're seeing kids this age all the time," Rosen says. There's no single explanation for the declining age of onset, although greater awareness on the part of parents certainly plays a role. Whatever the reason, these littlest patients, combined with new scientific research on the causes of anorexia, are pushing the clinical community—and families, and victims—to come up with new ways of thinking about and treating this devastating disease.

Not many years ago, the conventional wisdom held that adolescent girls "got" anorexia from the culture they lived in. Intense young women, mostly from white, wealthy families, were overwhelmed by pressure to be perfect from their suffocating parents, their demanding schools, their exacting coaches. And so they chose extreme dieting as a way to control their lives, to act out their frustration at never being perfect enough. In the past decade, though, psychiatrists have begun to see surprising diversity among their anorexic patients. Not only are anorexia's victims younger, they're also more likely to be black, Hispanic or Asian, more likely to be boys, more likely to be middle-aged. All of which caused doctors to question their core assumption: if anorexia isn't a disease of type-A girls from privileged backgrounds, then what is it?

Although no one can yet say for certain, new science is offering tantalizing clues. Doctors now compare anorexia to alcoholism and depression, potentially fatal diseases that may be set off by environmental factors such as stress or trauma, but have their roots in a complex combination of genes and brain chemistry. In other words, many kids are affected by pressure-cooker school environments and a culture of thinness promoted by magazines and music videos, but most of them don't secretly scrape their dinner into the garbage. The environment "pulls the trigger," says Cynthia Bulik, director of the eating-disorder program at the University of North Carolina at Chapel Hill. But it's a child's latent vulnerabilities that "load the gun."

Parents do play a role, but most often it's a genetic one. In the last 10 years, studies of anorexics have shown that the disease often runs in families. In a 2000 study published in *The American Journal of Psychiatry,* researchers at Virginia Commonwealth University studied 2,163 female twins and found that 77 of them suffered from symptoms of anorexia. By comparing the number of identical twins who had anorexia with the significantly smaller number of fraternal twins who had it, scientists concluded that more than 50 percent of the risk for developing the disorder could be attributed to an individual's genetic makeup. A few small studies have even isolated a specific area on the human genome where some of the mutations that may influence anorexia exist, and now a five-year, $10 million NIMH study is underway to further pinpoint the locations of those genes.

Amy Nelson, 14, a ninth grader from a Chicago suburb, thinks that genes played a role in her disease. Last year Amy's weight dropped from 105 to a skeletal 77 pounds, and her parents enrolled her in the day program at the Alexian Brothers Behavioral Health Hospital outside Chicago. Over the summer, as Amy was getting better, her father found the diary of his younger sister, who died at 18 of "unknown causes." In it, the teenager had calculated that she could lose 13 pounds in less than a month by restricting herself to less than 600 calories a day. No salt, no butter, no sugar, "not too many bananas," she wrote in 1980. "Depression can run in families," says Amy, "and an eating disorder is like depression. It's something wrong with your brain." These days, Amy is healthier and, though she doesn't weigh herself, thinks she's around 100. She has a part in the school play and is more casual about what she eats, even to the point of enjoying ice cream with friends.

Scientists are tracking important differences in the brain chemistry of anorexics. Using brain scans, researchers at the University of Pittsburgh, led by professor of psychiatry Dr. Walter Kaye, discovered that the level of serotonin activity in the brains of anorexics is abnormally high. Although normal levels of serotonin are believed to be associated with feelings of well-being, these pumped-up levels of hormones may be linked to feelings of anxiety and obsessional thinking, classic traits of anorexia. Kaye hypothesizes that anorexics use starvation as a mode of self-medication. How? Starvation prevents tryptophane, an essential amino acid that produces serotonin, from getting into the brain. By eating less, anorexics reduce the serotonin activity in their brains, says Kaye, "creating a sense of calm," even as they are about to die of malnutrition.

Almost everyone knows someone who has trouble with food: extremely picky eating, obsessive dieting, body-image problems, even voluntary vomiting are well known. But in the spectrum of eating disorders, anorexia, which affects about 2.5 million Americans, stands apart. For one thing, anorexics are often delusional. They can be weak with hunger while they describe physical sensations of overfullness that make it physically uncomfortable for them to swallow. They hear admonishing voices in their heads when they do manage to choke down a few morsels. They exercise compulsively, and even when they can count their ribs, their image in the mirror tells them to lose more.

When 12-year-old Erin Phillips, who lives outside Baltimore, was in her downward spiral, she stopped eating butter, then started eating with chopsticks, then refused solid food altogether, says her mother, Joann. Within two months, Erin's weight had slipped from 70 to 50 pounds. "Every day, I'd watch her melt away," Joann says. Before it struck her daughter, Joann had been dismissive about the disease. "I used to think the person should just eat something and get over it. But when you see it up close, you can't believe your eyes. They just can't." (Her confusion is natural: the term anorexia comes from a Greek word meaning "loss of appetite.")

Anorexia is a killer—it has the highest mortality rate of any mental illness, including depression. About half of anorexics get better. About 10 percent of them die. The rest remain chronically ill—exhausting, then bankrupting, parents, retreating from jobs and school, alienating friends as they struggle to manage the symptoms of their condition. Hannah Hartney of Tulsa, Okla., was first hospitalized with anorexia when she was 10. After eight weeks, she was returned to her watchful parents. For the last few years, she was able to maintain a normal weight but now, at 16, she's been battling her old demons again. "She's not out of the woods," says her mother, Kathryn.

While adults can drift along in a state of semi-starvation for years, the health risks for children under the age of 13 are dire. In their preteen years, kids should be gaining weight. During that critical period, their bones are thickening and lengthening, their hearts are getting stronger in order to pump blood to their growing bodies and their brains are adding mass, laying down new neurological pathways and pruning others—part of the explosion of mental and emotional development that occurs in those years. When children with eating disorders stop consuming sufficient calories, their bodies begin to conserve energy: heart

function slows, blood pressure drops; they have trouble staying warm. Whatever estrogen or testosterone they have in their bodies drops. The stress hormone cortisol becomes elevated, preventing their bones from hardening. Their
hair becomes brittle and falls out in patches. Their bodies begin to consume
muscle tissue. The brain, which depends at least in part on dietary fat to grow,
begins to atrophy. Unlike adult anorexics, children with eating disorders can
develop these debilitating symptoms within months.

Lori Cornwell says her son's descent was horrifyingly fast. In the summer
of 2004, 9-year-old Matthew Cornwell of Quincy, Ill., weighed a healthy 49
pounds. Always a picky eater, he began restricting his food intake until all he
would eat was a carrot smeared with a tablespoon of peanut butter. Within
three months, he was down to 39 pounds. When the Cornwells and their
doctor finally located a clinic that would accept a 10-year-old boy, Lori tucked
his limp body under blankets in the back seat of her car and drove all night
across the country. Matthew was barely conscious when he arrived at the
Children's Hospital in Omaha. "I knew that I had to get there before he
slipped away," she says.

With stakes this high, how do you treat a malnourished third grader who
is so ill she insists five Cheerios make a meal? First, say a growing number of
doctors and patients, you have to let parents back into the treatment process.
For more than a hundred years, parents have been regarded as an anorexic's
biggest problem, and in 1978, in her book "Golden Cage," psychoanalyst
Hilde Bruch suggested that narcissistic, cold and unloving parents (or, alterna-
tively, hypercritical, overambitious and overinvolved ones) actually caused the
disease by discouraging their children's natural maturation to adulthood.
Thirty years ago standard treatment involved helping the starving and often
delusional adolescents or young women to separate psychologically—and
sometimes physically—from their toxic parents. "We used to talk about
performing a parental-ectomy," says Dr. Ellen Rome, head of adolescent
medicine at the Cleveland Clinic.

Too often these days, parents aren't so much banished from the treatment
process as sidelined, watching powerlessly as doctors take what can be extreme
measures to make their children well. In hospitals, severely malnourished
anorexics are treated with IV drips and nasogastric tubes. In long-term residential treatment centers, an anorexic's food intake is weighed and measured,
bite by bite. In individual therapy, an anorexic tries to uncover the roots of
her obsession and her resistance to treatment. Most doctors use a combination
of these approaches to help their patients get better. Although parents are no
longer overtly blamed for their child's condition, says Marlene Schwartz, codi-
rector of the Yale eating-disorder clinic, doctors and therapists "give parents
the impression that eating disorders are something the parents did that the
doctors are now going to fix."

Worse, the state-of-the-art protocols don't work for many young children.
A prolonged stay in a hospital or treatment center can be traumatic. Talk therapy can help some kids, but many others are too young for it to be effective.

Back at home, family mealtimes become a nightmare. Parents, advised not to badger their child about food, say nothing—and then they watch helpless and heartbroken as their child pushes the food away.

In the last three years, some prominent hospitals and clinics around the country have begun adopting a new treatment model in which families help anorexics get better. The most popular of the home-based models, the Maudsley approach, was developed in the 1980s at the Maudsley Hospital in London. Two doctors there noticed that when severely malnourished, treatment-resistant anorexics were put in the hospital and fed by nurses, they gradually gained weight and began to participate in their own recovery. They decided that given the right support, family members could get anorexics to eat in the same way the nurses did. These days, family-centered therapy works like this: A team of doctors, therapists and nutritionists meets with parents and the child. The team explains that while the causes of anorexia are unclear, it is a severe, life-threatening disease like cancer or diabetes. Food, the family is told, is the medicine that will help the child get better. Like oncologists prescribing chemotherapy, the team provides parents with a schedule of calories, lipids, carbohydrates and fiber that the patient must eat every day and instructs them on how to monitor the child's intake. It coaches siblings and other family members on how to become a sympathetic support team. After a few practice meals in the hospital or doctor's office, the whole family is sent home for a meal.

"I told my daughter, 'You're going to hate this,'" says Mitzi Miles, whose daughter Kaleigh began struggling with anorexia at 10. "She said, 'I could never hate you, Mom.' And I said, 'We'll see.'" The first dinner at the Miles home outside Harrisburg, Pa., was a battle—but Mitzi, convinced by Kaleigh's doctor she was doing the right thing, didn't back down. After 45 minutes of yelling and crying, Kaleigh began to eat. Over the next 20 weeks, Kaleigh attended weekly therapy sessions, and Mitzi got support from the medical team, which instructed her to allow Kaleigh to make more food choices on her own. Eleven months later, Kaleigh is able to maintain a normal weight. Mitzi no longer measures out food portions or keeps a written log of her daily food intake.

Critics point out that the Maudsley approach won't work well for adults who won't submit to other people's making their food choices. And they charge that in some children, parental oversight can do more harm than good. Young anorexics and their parents are already locked in a battle for control, says Dr. Alexander Lucas, an eating-disorder specialist and professor emeritus at the Mayo Clinic in Minnesota. The Maudsley approach, he says, "may backfire" by making meals into a battleground. "The focus on weight gain," he says, "has to be between the physician and the child." Even proponents say that family-centered treatment isn't right for everyone: families where there is violence, sexual abuse, alcoholism or drug addiction aren't good candidates. But several studies both in clinics at the Maudsley Hospital and at the University of Chicago show promising results: five years after treatment, more than

70 percent of patients recover using the family-centered method, compared with 50 percent who recover by themselves or using the old approaches. Currently, a large-scale NIH study of the Maudsley approach is underway.

Mental-health specialists say the success of the family-centered approach is finally putting the old stigmas to rest. "An 8-year-old with anorexia isn't in a flight from maturity," says Dr. Julie O'Toole, medical director of the Kartini Clinic in Portland, Ore., a family-friendly eating-disorder clinic. "These young patients are fully in childhood." Most young anorexics, O'Toole says, have wonderful, thoughtful, terribly worried parents. These days, when a desperately sick child enters the Kartini Clinic, O'Toole tries to set parents straight. "I tell them it's a brain disorder. Children don't choose to have it and parents don't cause it." Then she gives the parents a little pep talk. She reminds them that mothers were once blamed for causing schizophrenia and autism until that so-called science was debunked. And that the same will soon be true for anorexia. At the conclusion of O'Toole's speech, she says, parents often weep.

Ironically, family dinners are one of the best ways to prevent a vulnerable child from becoming anorexic. Too often, dinner is eaten in the back seat of an SUV on the way to soccer practice. Parents who eat regular, balanced meals with their children model good eating practices. Family dinners also help parents spot any changes in their child's eating habits. Dieting, says Dr. Craig Johnson, director of the eating-disorder program at Laureate Psychiatric Hospital in Tulsa, triggers complex neurobiological reactions. If you have anorexia in the family and your 11-year-old tells you she's about to go on a diet and is thinking about joining the track team, says Johnson, "you want to be very careful about how you approach her request." For some kids, innocent-seeming behavior carries enormous risks.

Children predisposed to eating disorders are uniquely sensitive to media messages about dieting and health. And their interpretation can be starkly literal. When Ignatius Lau of Portland, Ore., was 11 years old, he decided that 140 pounds was too much for his 5-foot-2 frame. He had heard that oils and carbohydrates were fattening, so he became obsessed with food labels, cutting out all fats and almost all carbs. He lost 32 pounds in six months and ended up in a local hospital. "I told myself I was eating healthier," Ignatius says. He recovered, but for the next three years suffered frequent relapses. "I'd lose weight again and it would trigger some of my old behaviors, like reading food labels," he says. These days he knows what healthy feels like. Ignatius, now 17, is 5 feet 11, 180 pounds, and plays basketball.

Back in Richmond, Va., Emily Krudys says her family has changed. For two months Katherine stayed at the Omaha Children's Hospital, and slowly gained weight. Emily stayed nearby—attending the weekly therapy sessions designed to help integrate her into Katherine's treatment. After Katherine returned home, Emily home-schooled her while she regained her strength. This fall, Katherine entered sixth grade. She's got the pony, and she's become an avid horsewoman, sometimes riding five or six times a week. She's still slight, but she's gaining weight normally by eating three meals and three or four snacks a day. But the anxiety still lingers. When Katherine says she's hungry, Emily has been known to drop everything and whip up a three-course meal. The other day she was startled to see her daughter spreading sour cream on her potato. "I thought, 'My God, that's how regular kids eat all the time,'" she recalls. Then she realized that her daughter was well on the way to becoming one of those kids.

QUESTIONS

1. What is the new theory of the cause of anorexia? What prompted doctors to look for new ideas?

2. According to the newest theories, what is the strongest contribution parents make to the cause of their child's eating disorder?

3. How do people with anorexia use starvation as self-medication?

4. Why is it even more serious when a pre-teen develops anorexia than when an adult does?

14

Steroids: Youth at Risk

Steven Ungerleider

Several years ago, in a well-known research project, elite athletes were asked whether they would take a pill that guaranteed an Olympic gold medal if they knew it would kill them within a year. More than half of the athletes said they would take the pill.

The need to win at all costs has permeated many areas of our lives. In sports, one of the forms it takes is the use of anabolic-androgenic steroids (AAS). "Anabolic" refers to constructive metabolism or muscle-building, and "androgenic" means masculinizing. All AAS are derived from the hormone testosterone, which is found primarily in men, although women also produce it in smaller concentrations. There are at least thirty AAS, some natural and some synthetic.

Use of these substances has been pervasive for years among collegiate, Olympic, and professional competitors. Experiments with steroids began in Germany in the thirties, and their use by East German Olympic athletes is well known. More than 10,000 East German athletes in 22 events were given these synthetic hormones over 30 years. In August 2000, after a long battle in the criminal courts, more than 400 doctors, coaches, and trainers from the former East Germany were convicted of giving steroids to minors without their informed consent. But despite these revelations and convictions, scandals persist. Recently the chief of sports medicine for the United States Olympic Committee resigned in protest, saying that "some of our greatest Olympians have been using performance-enhancing drugs for years, and we have not been honest about our drug testing protocols."

Now anabolic steroids are becoming available to middle school and high school children as well. Concerns about body image and athletic performance lead adolescents to use the substances despite their serious side effects. Young athletes are responding to encouragement, social pressure, and their own desire to excel, as well as admonitions from coaches to put on muscle and build strength and resilience.

A recent survey by the National Institute on Drug Abuse indicates that steroid use by eighth- and tenth-graders is increasing, and twelfth-graders are increasingly likely to underestimate their risks. Some 2.7% of eighth- and tenth-graders and 2.9% of twelfth-graders admitted they had taken steroids at least once—a significant increase since 1991, the first year that full data were available. Other studies suggest that as many as 6% of high school students have used steroids. The numbers are especially alarming because many students will not admit that they take drugs. Sixth-graders report that these drugs are available in schoolyards, and they are increasingly used by nonathletes as well to impress their peers and attract the opposite sex.

Anabolic-androgenic steroids fall into three classes: C-17 alkyl derivatives of testosterone; esters or derivatives of 19-nortestosterone; and esters of testosterone.

C-17 alkyl derivatives are soluble in water and can be taken orally. Among them are Anavar, Anadrol, Dianabol (a favorite among Olympians), and the most famous, Winstrol, also known as stanozolol. Stanozolol was taken in large doses by the Canadian sprint champion Ben Johnson, who was stripped of a gold medal in the 1988 Olympics. These steroids are often favored by athletes trying to avoid drug screens because they clear the body quickly (within a month).

The 19-nortestosterone derivatives are oil-based; they are usually injected and absorbed into fat deposits, where long-term energy is stored. The most popular steroid in this group is nandrolone (Deca-Durabolin). It has recently made headlines because it is found in food supplements and other preparations that can be bought without a prescription. Many athletes who test positive for nandrolone say they had no idea what was in the vitamin supplements they took. Because nandrolone is stored in fatty tissue and released over a long period of time, it may take 8–10 months to clear the body.

Esters of testosterone, the third class, are especially dangerous. Among them are testosterone propionate, Testex, and cypionate. Active both orally and by injection, they closely mimic the effects of natural testosterone and are therefore difficult to detect on drug screens. The International Olympic Committee determines their presence by measuring the ratio of testosterone to the related substance epitestosterone in an athlete's urine; if the ratio exceeds 6:1, the athlete is suspected of cheating.

How do anabolic steroids work? The scientific literature demonstrates their effects, but it is not clear how they enhance the synthesis of proteins and the growth of muscles. They apparently increase endurance, allowing longer periods of exercise, and improve the results of strength training by increasing both the size (mass) of muscles and the number of muscle fibers.

Especially when taken in high doses, AAS can induce irritability and aggression. When Hitler's SS troops took steroids to build strength and stave off fatigue, they found that the hormones also made them more fearless and willing to fight. Among young athletic warriors today, steroids not only permit harder training and faster recovery from long workouts but may also induce a sense of invincibility and promote excessively macho behavior—and occasionally, attacks of rage or psychosis.

These drugs have a great many other risks as well. Men may develop reduced sperm production, shrunken testicles, impotence, and irreversible breast enlargement. Women may develop deep voices and excessive body hair. In either sex, baldness and acne are risks. The ratio of good to bad lipids may change, increasing the danger of heart attacks, strokes, and liver cancer. In adolescents bone growth may stop prematurely. (See Table for details on side effects). Injecting steroids with contaminated needles creates a risk of HIV and other blood-borne infections.

Mental health professionals must consider how to address this problem in our schools. The National Institute on Drug Abuse and its nongovernmental partners have established Web sites to educate youth about the dangers of steroids. These sites may be found at steroidabuse.org, archpediatrics.com, and drugabuse.gov. A useful site for professionals interested in intervention

---

Side Effects of Anabolic-Androgenic Steroids

In men:
- Gynecomastia (breast development), usually permanent
- Testicular or scrotal pain
- Testicular atrophy and decreased sperm production
- Premature baldness, even in adolescents
- Enlargement of the prostate gland, causing difficult urination

In women:
- Enlargement of the clitoris, usually irreversible
- Disruption of the menstrual cycle
- Permanent deepening of the voice
- Excessive facial and body hair

In both sexes:
- Nervous tension
- Aggressiveness and antisocial behavior
- Paranoia and psychotic states
- Acne, often serious enough to leave permanent scars on the face and body
- Burning and pain during urination
- Gastrointestinal and leg muscle cramps
- Headaches
- Dizziness
- High blood pressure
- Heart, kidney, and liver damage
- In adolescents, premature end to the growth of long bones, leading to shortened stature

---

and prevention is tpronline.org. Researchers at the Oregon Health Sciences University have devised an effective program known as Adolescents Training and Learning to Avoid Steroids (ATLAS). It is a team-centered and gender-specific approach that educates athletes about the dangers of steroids and other drugs while providing alternatives including nutritional advice and strength training. A three-year study demonstrated the benefits of the program for 3,000 football players in 31 Oregon high schools. ATLAS reduced not only anabolic steroid use but also alcohol and illicit drug use and drunk driving. Still more research is needed both to address the potentially deadly consequences of youthful steroid use and to discover ways of preventing it.

Steven Ungerleider, Ph.D., is a clinical psychologist and an adjunct professor at the University of Oregon who regularly consults with the U.S. Olympic Committee. He can be reached at the Web site shorel.com or at suinteg@attglobal.net.

QUESTIONS

1. What are the reasons middle and high school students use steroids, despite the significant risks involved?

2. What is ATLAS? What features of ATLAS seem to contribute to the success of the approach in educating youth about the dangers of steroid use?

3. How may coaches unintentionally contribute to decisions by young athletes to use steroids?

The Cruelest Cut: Often It's the One Teens Inflict on Themselves

Why Are So Many American Kids Secretly Self-Mutilating?

Jeffrey Kluger

Byline: Jeffrey Kluger/Cambridge

Vanessa's arms no longer show the damage she once did to them. That's saying something, given that the damage was considerable. The college freshman, 19, started with just a few scratches from a sharp piece of plastic. Later came the razor blades and then the kitchen knives. After a time, she took to wearing bracelets to cover her injuries; when that wasn't enough, she began cutting less conspicuous parts of her body. "I was very creative," she says, with a smile.

Vanessa needn't be so clever anymore. In the past 18 months, she has cut herself only once. She was pleased and surprised to find that she didn't enjoy it a bit.

For most people—and especially most parents—the idea that anyone would tolerate the sting of a razor blade or the cut of a knife, much less enjoy it, is unthinkable. But maybe they are just not paying attention. Vanessa is not a member of some remote fringe of the emotionally disabled but part of a growing population of boys and girls for whom cutting, burning or otherwise self-injuring is becoming a common—if mystifying—way of managing emotional pain.

Nobody knows how many cutters are at large, but psychologists have been conducting surveys and gathering data from clinics, hospitals and private practices, and they are shocked by what they are finding. According to one study in the *Journal of Abnormal Psychology,* from 14% to 39% of adolescents engage in self-mutilative behavior. That range is suspiciously broad, and other estimates have put the figure at just 6% or below. But with more than 70 million American kids out there, that's still an awful lot of routine—and secret—self-mutilation. "Every clinician says it's increasing," reports psychologist Michael Hollander, a director at Two Brattle Center in Cambridge, Mass., an outpatient clinic that treats cutters. "I've been practicing for 30 years, and I think it's gone up dramatically."

The good news is that even as the population of cutters grows, so does the legion of professionals working on new ways to unravel and treat the problem. The first step is to understand why kids do this to themselves.

Overwhelmingly, self-mutilators say they began cutting for one of two reasons: to feel less or to feel more. Some kids suffering from such problems as anxiety, depression or borderline-personality disorder—a condition characterized by explosiveness and unstable relationships—find their pain so overwhelming that they simply shut off their emotional spigot. Cutting, they find, is a way to kick-start feelings when the numbness becomes worse than the pain. Other kids say the opposite—that their emotional turmoil is so great that they need something to serve as a bleed valve to calm them down in times of crisis. "I would do it when things got me upset," says Brittany, 17, an outpatient at the Vista Del Mar clinic in west Los Angeles. "At the time it was a relief, until you wake up the next morning, look at your arms and think, s___, what did I do?"

The population of kids who wake up this way is becoming increasingly diverse. The stereotypical cutter is a girl in her young teens suffering from discord at home and doing poorly at school, and there is some truth to that cliche. "Girls have a more conflicted relationship with their bodies," says Wendy Lader, clinical director of Self Abuse Finally Ends, a treatment program in Naperville, Ill. "They go after it and hurt it when they're angry." While such traumas as sexual abuse don't always precede cutting, they often do appear to be risk factors.

But cutting is becoming an increasingly democratized disorder. By some estimates, up to 30% of self-mutilators are boys, and many cutters of both sexes come from apparently stable, two-parent homes in which there is no evidence of abuse. Some of the kids have a history of suicide attempts, but many have no interest in ending their lives, no matter how self-destructive their behavior seems to be. How often they injure themselves generally depends on how acute the underlying psychological pain is. In one study, kids self-mutilated anywhere from once to 745 times a year. "They do it because it works better than anything else they've tried," says Hollander.

Few researchers doubt that there is a certain trendiness to cutting and that that is driving the numbers up. Celebrities including Angelina Jolie and Fiona

Apple have confessed to past self-mutilation. Though it's true that such public disclosures encourage ordinary kids to come forward, it's also true that when glamorous people suffer from something, a bit of the glitter rubs off on the condition. "Cutting grew into a huge fad at school," says Michelle, 13, who is being treated at the Vista Del Mar clinic. "In seventh grade it seemed every single girl had tried it—except the really smart ones." Then there is the Internet, where cutting chat rooms are just a keystroke away. Many offer support for kids who want to stop, but just as many wink at the problem and even subtly encourage it.

The neurological roots of cutting are a mystery, but several theories have been put forward. When the body is injured, it releases natural opiates that help dull pain—a process that is behind the fabled runner's high. Cutting inflicts a very real injury, and self-mutilators may be seeking the neurochemical kick that follows. "When I would cut myself deliberately, I didn't even feel it," says Emily, 16, who is in her third week of treatment at Two Brattle Center. "But if I got a paper cut I didn't want, that would hurt."

The problem is that any time you chase a high, you risk getting hooked on it. "The longer kids cut, the more they need it," says psychologist Jennifer Hartstein of the Montefiore Medical Center in Bronx, N.Y., where Vanessa was treated.

Overcoming self-mutilation turns out to be less tricky than explaining it. Perhaps the most effective treatment is dialectical behavior therapy (DBT). Developed by psychologist Marsha Linehan of the University of Washington in Seattle, DBT is used as a frontline therapy for borderline-personality disorder. Because there appears to be a very significant overlap between borderlines and cutters, Linehan and others wondered if the same treatment might work equally well for both. It does.

DBT is built around the idea of encouraging the cutters and members of their family to accept the kids as they are while encouraging them to change. "We embrace two seemingly contradictory philosophies," says Hartstein. "That teens are doing the best they can and that they can also do more." With the sense of judgment lifted, children are more receptive to learning a wide range of new coping skills, such as impulse control, distress tolerance and contemplation of consequences.

The treatment at Two Brattle Center is typical of what's offered at most clinics. Cutters start with intensive DBT and coping training, attending sessions from 9 a.m. to 1 p.m., five days a week, for at least four weeks. When they are ready, they graduate to individual and group therapy, once a week each. All the kids have paging privileges, giving them a round-the-clock hotline to their therapists when the urge to cut hits. They are also taught to reach out to family and friends and answer the cutting impulse with some other activity.

"When Melanie wanted to cut, she learned to find something else to do," says the father of a 20-year-old Two Brattle graduate. "She'd be stressed, and the next thing we'd know, she'd be cleaning her closet."

Parents who are worried that their kids are cutting should look for a few red flags. If a teen wears long sleeves and sweatpants in hot weather, there's a chance something is being hidden. Temperamental behavior, intense anger and changes in eating and sleeping patterns may also be warning signals—but they are also part of the ordinary storms of adolescence, so it's wise not to overinterpret. Less ambiguous are sudden shifts in mood. "If a kid is mopey at 5 and much better at 5:30," says Hartstein, "you may want to know what happened in that half-hour." Parents should also keep an eye out for hidden stashes of blades or bandages.

More important than advice for parents is advice for the kids. Almost all former self-mutilators agree that one of the best things cutters can do is come forward—talk about their problems with parents, teachers and friends. It's equally critical for the kids to talk honestly with themselves. "Take a step back," advises Jen, 17, a Two Brattle patient. "Look at the long term. Who's in control of your life, the cutting or you?" Self-mutilation may thrive on secrecy and fear, but as with all wounds, a little fresh air can help speed the healing.—With reporting by Jeffrey Ressner/Los Angeles.

QUESTIONS

1. What purpose does self-injury serve for cutters?
2. What are the stereotypical traits of a cutter?
3. How can cutting become addictive?
4. What is the most effective treatment for cutting? How is it done?

InfoMarks: Make Your Mark

What Is an InfoMark?

It is a single-click return ticket to any page, any result, or any search from InfoTrac College Edition.

An InfoMark is a stable URL, linked to InfoTrac College Edition articles that you have selected. InfoMarks can be used like any other URL, but they're better because they're stable—they don't change. Using an InfoMark is like performing the search again whenever you follow the link, whether the result is a single article or a list of articles.

How Do InfoMarks Work?

If you can "copy and paste," you can use InfoMarks.

When you see the InfoMark icon on a result page, its URL can be copied and pasted into your electronic document—web page, word processing document, or email. Once InfoMarks are incorporated into a document, the results are persistent (the URLs will not change) and are dynamic.

Even though the saved search is used at different times by different users, an InfoMark always functions like a brand new search. Each time a saved search is executed, it accesses the latest updated information. That means subsequent InfoMark searches might yield additional or more up-to-date information than the original search with less time and effort.

Capabilities

InfoMarks are the perfect technology tool for creating:

- Virtual online readers
- Current awareness topic sites—links to periodical or newspaper sources
- Online/distance learning courses
- Bibliographies, reference lists
- Electronic journals and periodical directories
- Student assignments
- Hot topics

Advantages

- Select from over 15 million articles from more than 5,000 journals and periodicals
- Update article and search lists easily
- Articles are always full-text and include bibliographic information
- All articles can be viewed online, printed, or emailed
- Saves professors and students time
- Anyone with access to InfoTrac College Edition can use it
- No other online library database offers this functionality
- FREE!

How to Use InfoMarks

There are three ways to utilize InfoMarks—in HTML documents, Word documents, and Email.

HTML Document

1. Open a new document in your HTML editor (Netscape Composer or FrontPage Express).
2. Open a new browser window and conduct your search in InfoTrac College Edition.
3. Highlight the URL of the results page or article that you would like to InfoMark.
4. Right-click the URL and click Copy. Now, switch back to your HTML document.
5. In your document, type in text that describes the InfoMarked item.
6. Highlight the text and click on Insert, then on Link in the upper bar menu.
7. Click in the link box, then press the "Ctrl" and "V" keys simultaneously and click OK. This will paste the URL in the box.
8. Save your document.

Word Document

1. Open a new Word document.
2. Open a new browser window and conduct your search in InfoTrac College Edition.
3. Check items you want to add to your Marked List.
4. Click on Mark List on the right menu bar.
5. Highlight the URL, right-click on it, and click Copy. Now, switch back to your Word document.
6. In your document, type in text that describes the InfoMarked item.
7. Highlight the text. Go to the upper bar menu and click on Insert, then on Hyperlink.

8. Click in the hyperlink box, then press the "Ctrl" and "V" keys simultaneously and click OK. This will paste the URL in the box.
9. Save your document.

Email

1. Open a new email window.
2. Open a new browser window and conduct your search in InfoTrac College Edition.
3. Highlight the URL of the results page or article that you would like to InfoMark.
4. Right-click the URL and click Copy. Now, switch back to your email window.
5. In the email window, press the "Ctrl" and "V" keys simultaneously. This will paste the URL into your email.
6. Send the email to the recipient. By clicking on the URL, he or she will be able to view the InfoMark.